How to Thrive in the New Healthcare Economy

Direct Access, POPTS, Hospital Systems and Insurance Companies

CHAD MADDEN

Killer Marketing Secrets

Contributor: Carl Mattiola

Book & Cover Design: IF Design Graphic Design & Photography, Ida Fia Sveningsson Konsult

ISBN-13: 978-1535434386
ISBN-10: 1535434384
ASIN: B01JGLL5O8

Table of Content

Chapter 1

My Story and How We Got Here

More Than You'll Ever Want to Know About Me...
and My Private Practice Story...

This is Chapter One...which is my scattered story and my purpose for writing this book for you.

(Don't worry...the rest of the book will be a bit more focused)...

Flashback to September 2, 2003...My wife, Stephanie, was literally 9 months pregnant with my son, Jackson.

September 2, 2003 is also the day that I opened my private practice, Madden Physical Therapy, here in Harrisburg, Pennsylvania.

Previously I had been a Clinical Director.

The reason that I was opening my own private practice was because I was served a nonchalant non-compete about 6 months into employment there.

So my wife was 6 months pregnant and I just had it in my head...this thought that just stuck with me...

It was: "If I don't open a practice, if I don't go into business for myself before my oldest son was born, I probably never was going to do it."

So I kind of felt some pressure.

My wife was about to deliver...

I had also taken somewhat a cut in pay initially to be the Clinical Director... and now here I was trying to completely replace her income.

Just to give you the whole history of my physical therapy career, I graduated with an MSPT, a Master's Degree in Physical Therapy, from Misericordia in May of 2000.

Prior to working as a Clinical Director in a private practice group, I worked in a POPTS practice, an orthopedic surgery group.

I was there for about 2 years, mainly just honing my skills as a Physical Therapist.

It was a really good position for me to learn.

The reason why it was good for me to learn is because it didn't really matter how I did as a clinician...there was just an endless source of referrals coming down from upstairs. (That's scary, huh?!)

But I did care...and even early on it was important to me that the patients got better...

It was a good environment for me to learn that.

So there are pluses and minuses with a POPTS practices for a new grad—for me it was great.

Anyhow, fast forward to September 1, 2003...

This is the eve of me opening my private practice.

It was Labor Day...a holiday.

My parents were there, and my in-laws, and my wife (again, being nine months pregnant).

She was in the suite helping me clean, helping me get ready for the first day.

We had five new patients lined up for the first day.

I just remember there was a point where she said, "Hey, I just need a minute."

I remember she was standing there leaning against a wall...and it just kind of hit me, "Oh shit..I better make this work."

The other part of the story that you should know about is three months before when I first stated, "Yes, I was going to go into business for myself"... I was out to either lunch or dinner with my parents and my wife, Stephanie.

There was a conversation amongst the four of us that this was bad timing.

Guess what? It was bad timing...

But I just want to give them full credit for doing this - once they knew that I was committed to the vision and opening up, they were 100% supportive.

I don't think I will ever forget that vision of her standing there, leaning against the wall, just saying, "I need a minute," because she was trying to help me get ready for the next day.

I carried that with me... "Wow, this is serious. This isn't a test run. I really better make things happen here."

Chapter 1

In the beginning, opening up, like most Private Practice owners in the beginning...I didn't know what I didn't know.

I didn't know that I had no idea how to handle personnel.

I didn't know the ins and outs of financing.

And I had no idea how to market, especially as a private practice owner.

When I was working in the POPTS clinic, they would just keep referring patients down regardless of how good or bad I did.

Luckily, when I worked for the POPTS...I had some good relationships with the physicians upstairs, who also happened to own the practice and who I was an employee for...they would refer literally a ton of patients to me.

Patients would come downstairs with my name on the script.

That was great, but now here I was out on my own...

There was no financial incentive for them to send to me anymore and I had no idea how to market.

> I didn't know personnel.
> I didn't know financing.
> I didn't know marketing.

They are basically the three pillars of any business, let alone a private practice Physical Therapist who was now out on his own for the first time.

The one thing that I did know was how to write a business plan just because I had done it before and I had dreamed about being in business for myself... I think from the time I was sixteen or seventeen years old.

I even shared in PT school that I wanted to do that.

Again, I didn't know what I didn't know yet...but I knew how to write a business plan and I knew that the most important part of the business plan was the pro forma - that is the forecast of what the income and the expenses would look like.

Within ninety days, I had a bank line of credit.

So within ninety days of making the decision to go into private practice for myself, I had a line of credit...for $50,000.

That is what I started my private practice on...a shoestring budget.

I think I had maybe $6,000 in the bank, which was two months of living expenses for my wife and I at that time.

That's it...that's all I had.

Again, there was even more pressure on me to make this work.

I didn't really have five years to do a break-even...I had to make it work pretty quick.

"Did You Get Your 5 This Week?"

My original business plan, my first one, was actually with one of the orthopedic surgeons that had left the group that I worked for, he went independent. He was actually going to rent a room to me in his office.

Luckily, HealthSouth came in and blocked me from going into the building. So that was really cool... HealthSouth was already in the building.

I thought it was a huge barrier at the time, but they ended up doing me a huge favor because I had to go out and be completely independent.

I also knew with my original business plan, that I needed five new patients a week.

The way that my pro forma worked, my forecast was that if I had five new patients a week and I factored in a really low attendance rate (I think it was 80% at the time, which is anemic)... and an average length of stay of ten visits... I knew that Steph could stay at home - my wife who was about to deliver.

So she could stay at home and I still could double my salary of what I was making before and I would replace her salary so that she could raise our oldest son.

Our oldest son was born that Friday.

Let me give you the timeline again...

Monday was Labor Day, so that is where I am cleaning and getting set up.

Tuesday was my first day open. I had five new patients that day, which was almost a miracle because that is exactly what the business plan called for.

Then that Friday, Jackson was born.

Obviously I did not treat that day on Friday.

I think I was a bad enough husband and father at the time that I even went back to work on Monday, at least for a few hours...pretty insensitive, right?

The one thing that I remember, especially early on... every night that I would come home, Steph would say, "Did you get your five?"

Meaning did I have enough business coming in to support us. Did I get my five new patients that week?

Some weeks we would get our five by Wednesday or Tuesday even.

Other weeks I would go in there Friday morning and I would have three new patients on the week.

That was really important to me.

By the way, just to give you a timeline or a time reference, this was before Direct Access in Pennsylvania and really the only way to function was to get referrals from physicians. Most of the physicians that I had known in the three years of my physical therapy profession up to that point, had their own PT practice. So they weren't going to refer to me.

Didn't Know What I Didn't Know Yet...

What I ended up doing was 37 luncheons in the first four months of private practice, because I knew nothing else.

> I had no idea how to market.
> I had no idea how to do marketing direct to the public.
> I had no idea how to market to physicians and pretty much what I would get would be the mercy referrals.

It was an absolute disaster.

I ended up spilling General Tso sauce all over the back of my beat up gray Saturn SL that I had from college... but I would hustle and I would get those mercy referrals.

Again, there were other things that I did not know that were coming into play,

I don't want to date myself, but I remember the Hershey factory went from a $5 copay to a $10 copay per visit. That was a really big stink. That was front page news in our local paper that the copay was going from $5 to $10 for these workers.

Now we are way past that... but I didn't know the insurance changes that were on the horizon.

I didn't know that POPTS practices would become a really, really big deal - especially here in Central Pennsylvania.

I didn't know that hospital systems would begin looking for other ways (with their declining reimbursement) to completely overtake the family physicians market and employ 70% of the referral sources in the local area.

I didn't see those changes coming.

I didn't know that corporate physical therapy companies would begin buying almost every private practice, not only in my area, but in the surrounding area and having really, really heavy competition.

I didn't foresee those things coming.

My only thing was did I get my five referrals a week?

On a positive note, I didn't know that Direct Access was coming either at the time... that definitely wasn't a sure thing in 2003.

My ignorance led to one quarter in 2007...the fourth quarter in 2007...I lost $43,000.

You would have thought I learned my lesson there... but again, two years later in the fourth quarter of 2009, I ended up losing nearly $100,000 ($98,000 plus).

I didn't realize at that time that my biggest struggles would lead to my biggest wins.

Now we run a promotion that I will talk about here later in the book called, My Greatest Promotion Ever.

That is a promotion that we do in October or November of every year that now gives us a huge backlog of patients to see...through our typical slow season...It is really, really cool.

Other things that I didn't know... I didn't know that I would lose my top referral source three different times.

I will quickly share those with you:

1. The orthopedic surgeon that was going to rent me a room (almost six months to the date after I opened), ended up moving to Arizona because there were major changes to malpractice insurance in Pennsylvania. It almost doubled or tripled overnight. So he took his young family and moved to Arizona where he is doing really well right now. I think he represented almost 25% of my referral base at the time.

2. The second time was from an unethical issue with a referral source. He asked me to do something unethical. I refused to do it. He went from referring a high of, I think his peak was 86 patients in a year to zero overnight.

3. The third one was just here recently where we had a family physician who was our top referral source and admired us so much that he turned around and opened his own POPTS practice, his own physical therapy practice. Yikes!

I have gone on to survive that three times. Every time that that has happened, it has forced us to look at our marketing, strengthen it, learn how to transition away from physician referral and do more Direct Access marketing to the general public.

Now we incorporate something called the 4% rule:

We don't want any referral source being more than 4% of our total referral base.

I'm not really looking for the physician who is looking to enter into a perverse relationship with me and refer 5-10 new patients a week.

That is not what we are looking for.

We are looking for physicians referring to us for the right reasons.

We want to be really, really wide.

Since 2007, 8 consecutive years running, we have had two hundred referral sources in any given year because of that 4% rule and because of those huge losses leading to our biggest wins.

The other thing that it forced me to do is study a ton of marketing.

I have taken the same courses that we are all marketed to through the APTA, the PPS, and the other private organizations that offer marketing help... not only within private practice PT, but I found my biggest wins were looking outside of physical therapy.

Specifically... I can give you an example... I really got into direct response marketing.

You may affiliate or associate Dan Kennedy with direct response marketing.

I literally just sat down and read, I think, almost all of his books (I think he has 20 or 21 books published).

The way that I got to Dan...and Direct Response Marketing...was watching a testimonial of an orthodontist in Kansas.

His name is Dr. Dustin Burleson.

I was listening to what he was saying and he just happened to casually mention, "Hey, we do all direct response marketing that Dan Kennedy and GKIC promote."

I had never heard of that, so it forced me to swim upstream a little bit and begin studying Dan Kennedy.

Dr. Burleson is an awesome guy. He has an absolutely amazing, growing, thriving orthodontic practice in a highly competitive area out in Kansas.

The other thing that I got from him: I just studied and learned from him how he shares his information and shortcuts and success secrets with other orthodontists.

He is actually one of the trailblazers that I modeled off of for exactly what I am doing here...sharing what works and what doesn't work in successfully running a Private Practice.

Having done that... having gotten knocked down and learned a valuable lesson from the school of hard knocks... and then going out and studying, is greatly motivating and very rewarding.

We hit a point where in 30 consecutive months, we had 600% growth.

Just to give you an idea, let's say you are doing 400 visits a month right now.

So that would be like a year from now going to 800 visits a month.

And then a year from then, going to 1,600 visits a month and continuing to grow for the next six months at that same rate.

What that would be is going from 400 to 2,400 visits a month, just to give you an idea.

We went through that, almost those numbers exactly.

I know in the beginning... when we first start out with private practice and we open our own door and we put our name on our building or the name that we find is going to leave the biggest impact...we all have this viewpoint of how we are going to change the world.

I know that in the entrepreneurial journey, or the private practice owner journey, we all start off with some sort of jadedness...

We have seen things done a way that we don't approve of...that we don't like.

I know one specific thing at one place I worked for - they would use the same electrical stim pads on every single patient. I thought that was absolutely gross.

So when I opened my own practice, I would just get cases of e-stim pads.

(We don't even use e-stim very much anymore. It is less than a 1% incidence rate unless it is ordered by the physician.)

But at the time, it was really important to me... that focus on cleanliness, just because I very much valued that.

I came in a bit jaded, and I think most of us do...if we search far enough we have those same exact stories of when we were working for someone else and we were thinking, "I would do things different."

And we do go out and do that...but what happens is, we go out and we are doing that and we get knocked on our tail because we don't know what we don't know yet...

We suffer a loss. Maybe a physician referral source moves away or we have an income loss. Or we are panicked on a Thursday night about how we are ever going to make payroll the next day.

We have to go through the experience and figure that out.

Usually, the second step in that process, after we have our big dream, is we begin to compromise.

We say, "If I just made X amount of dollars. If I just made this much money, then it would be all worth it."

Most of us figure that out.

After we figure that out, we say, "Ok, now we are making great money, but we are working 70 hours a week. And that kind of sucks. So I'm basically working two full-time jobs, but I'm making good money."

Then we get to the point of... "If we just had systems in place then we would have enough time, enough time to pursue other interests. We would have enough time to invest in our family. We would have enough time to work on our business."

That is kind of the third stage, the third step.

By the way, I will cover this more in a later chapter on The 4 Levels of Private Practice PT... but I think it important to understand this entrepreneurial journey.

I had done that. I had gone through the route.

I had gotten to the point where we had three full-time teams. We were doing over 450 visits a week on average. Things were running pretty much without me. I could just be here five hours a week of admin time and market time and our practice would run.

I came back to a little bit of soul searching, looking for that life purpose.

What I was convinced about was... I was going to do commercial real estate, which at that point, I had built up to a 6 million dollar real estate portfolio.

When I hit 10 million dollars, the way my calculations worked, I would be pretty much financially free.

That was pretty much the plan, until I got a cold email from a gentleman who you will learn more about here.

His name is Carl Mattiola.

Carl, at the time, was working for Tesla and he was responsible for setting up their online sales division.

If you have ever read about Mary Beth Moore, who is Elon Musk's personal assistant... Carl would get calls from Mary Beth Moore that Elon wanted this project done. Then he would have to work furiously 24/7 with his team for the next 60 days just executing this thing that Elon wanted.

What he started to do was he wanted to use his IT skills to help Physical Therapists.

Carl was in the process... this was early, early on before there was Breakthrough PT Marketing, before there was ClinicMetrics, before there was ClinicRise... he was sending out cold emails to practice owners.

The sole purpose was just to interview.

So we set up a 15 minute call.

I told him I didn't have enough time... you know how we are as private practice owners... I had no time at all.

I said, "By the way, if you try to pitch me something and don't let me know ahead of time, I'm just going to hang up and we are going to be done."

He promised that wasn't the case and he just wanted to talk.

He proceeded with probably the best 15 minute interview/ survey that I had ever seen.

I said, "I have been studying marketing for a while, what are you doing?"

He shared with me, "I'm at Tesla and I live here in San Francisco. Every day I get up at 6AM and I talk with private practice owners for 3 hours before I go to work. I'm interested in physical therapy. I want to use my skill set to help Physical Therapists. I just want to know... what are your biggest pains?"

I was like wow, that is really, really cool.

From that conversation, he ended up starting a company, founding a company called ClinicMetrics.

Within a year, he left his job at Tesla. (He left a lot of money on the table. I'll let him speak to that.)

He started this company called ClinicMetrics.

What happened is, as he was surveying private practice owners all over the US - about "what are our biggest barriers?"...

One is we don't know our numbers.

Two is we have trouble marketing. We don't know how to market.

What ended up coming out of that is anytime he would reach a private practice owner who had this big pain of not knowing how to market their private practice, he would just do an email introduction of "there is this private practice owner in Harrisburg, Pennsylvania who is crushing it in a really competitive market, you should talk with him. He has figured out Direct Access marketing and you should talk with him."

He would do this email introduction... Guess what?

I had no idea how to share my information.

I kind of ignored the opportunity a little bit.

I would talk with the owner. I would give them a 30 minute or one hour phone call and the conversation would really go nowhere.

I didn't really know how to transfer what I was doing. I didn't know how to hold them accountable so that they actually implemented it. It was just kind of like I didn't have a high level of interest.

Basically, I stunk at it.

Shortly thereafter, in 2013, I was with one of my mentors...

As you will learn, I have 3 mentors. This mentor's name is Ernie.

Ernie is a fascinating gentleman. He is in his early 80's now... he started to have some health issues.

He is a huge sports fan, so this is NBA finals time... I hadn't been to an NBA game in 20 years. I'm not sure I will go to another game.

But we had the opportunity to go to Game 6 of the 2013 NBA Finals between the Miami Heat and the San Antonio Spurs... we went to the game.

This was the game where Ray Allen hit the 3 in the corner. We were like 20 rows up from Ray Allen, right behind Lenny Kravitz. So we saw Shaq, we saw Stephen A. Smith, Chris Webber... all of these people were right around us.

We had amazing seats - we saw Ray Allen hit the 3 and send the game into overtime.

The Heat were down 7 points with 43 seconds left to play...the crowd had started to file out of the American Airlines Arena. The Heat completed a furious comeback with Ray Allen hitting the 3 in the corner to tie it up...

Miami went on to win Game 6 in overtime... and won Game 7 and the Championship.

Most people thought the Spurs were going to win it...but they had to wait another year until 2014 to get another Championship.

Half of American Airlines Arena had emptied out and we stayed and watched the game finish. It was absolutely amazing that we had that experience.

Then on the way home, we are on the flight together and Ernie leaned over and said, "So what are you going to do now?"

I was kind of at a vulnerable point and I said, "Well, I'm really thinking... I have had a couple of offers to sell my practice. I don't think that I am going to do that. I want it to keep running like it is now. I just want to do commercial real estate - maybe buy one or two more buildings and then I will pretty much be financially set."

He said, "So what are you going to do?"

I said, "Well, I think I just said."

He said, "That will be a shame. You know you have this information. You have really good stuff to share with other private practice owners. For you to not share that, I think you are making a big mistake. How old are you?"

I think I was 36 or 37 at the time.

He said, "You have got a lot of stuff to share. It is time for you to figure out how to share it."

That was the end of the conversation.

It just kind of planted a seed with me... I didn't agree or disagree with him at the time, but it planted a seed.

Fast forward again a couple of months after that...

Now I was trying to figure out how to work with practice owners... some successes, some failures.

Carl and I had a phone call and I said, "Hey, you are on the phone with all of these owners, why don't I just license all of these things that I am doing to you and you can sell them and I will just get a licensing fee or a royalty fee on the backend. I don't even care what it is. I think you know how to do this and I don't. I'm not sure I want to put the effort into learning how to do it. I probably could do it if I wanted to, but I want you to think about licensing everything that I do and sharing it."

He said, "No."
He didn't even think about it. He said it right away. He just said no...
He said, "You need to learn how to do this."

So I did.

It is a pretty disturbing story, but what I ended up doing is buying a course. It is called an Information Marketing Course that walked me through basically 90 days of how to learn more about the people that I was trying to serve.

Even though I am a private practice owner, I only had my reality and what has been real for me and what has worked and what has not worked for me in my practice.

I learned how to talk to other private practice owners and find out what that pain is and also offer a solution that they can replicate and implement in their private practices and get huge wins out of it.

So that was really, really cool...

Once I learned how to do that – and by the way, how I learned was I took this course and I woke up every day at 3:50AM and I would run for 30 minutes, and then I would lock myself in a sauna for 3 hours.

I studied this course for 21 days in a row until I made it through. I did all of the exercises and just started implementing it. It has been a rocket ride since then...

We are now sharing information with over 200 practices all over the US and also now in Australia, Physios in Australia, and we just picked up a Physio in Malaysia. It has been an absolute rocket ride.

I'm just really honored that I get to help other people and that I have been put in that position of responsibility.

Again, just really honored and I consider it a privilege every day that I get to talk to other practice owners and get to help them.

Now, before I start sharing some really cool stuff (hopefully that you haven't seen before), I want to tell you who this is for and who it is not for.

Let's start with who this book is NOT for...

If you are in a POPTS practice, if you are a Physical Therapist working in a hospital system, if you are outside of private practice PT, this book is probably not for you.

I'm going to explain.

I'm going to share some really good stuff in this book, but it is very much geared towards private practice Physical Therapists. We have had interactions with everybody from Massage Therapists, personal trainers, Chiropractors, Physical Therapists in hospitals systems, POPTS practices, etc. trying to get into the course that we do.

My true purpose is to work strictly with private practice owners.

Because of this, we have made efforts to set up screenings so we can know exactly who we are working with...and the Rule is Private Practice PTs only.

So that is where my passion lies.

Also, if you are looking for a winning lotto ticket and you want somebody to cash this in for you and you know that you have a history of non-implementation, the book probably isn't for you.

The other thing is if you are in a bad partnership or if you are outside of private practice PT... what is going to happen is I'm going to give you some really good ideas in here. You are probably going to look for more information and I'm likely just not going to be able to give you that advanced information.

I have worked with one too many practices where one owner is all on board with growth and has a big vision and wants to do great things... and the other one is a stick in the mud and just doesn't want to grow. They tend to just be very conservative, very negative and just aren't ready to grow.

They usually have had some history of loss meaning they took a course that promised big things and they felt in the end that they didn't get their money's worth and they wasted their money.

By the way, as practice owners, we have all had those experiences. I know I have.

Anyhow, if you are in one of those situations, this book probably isn't for you.

Now... who is it for?

There are 5 things that I look for when working with an owner that I am sharing my top notch stuff with:

1. Ideally they are in private practice PT because that is where I am at and it is the easiest person for me to relate to.

2. They have a big dream. They don't want to settle for the status quo. They are aspiring to be something bigger than where they are at right now.

3. They use evidence-based practice. They have a high quality of care within the clinic and they really care about their patients getting better.

4. They are a life-long learner and they have great work ethic.

5. They are willing to take responsibility for anything that happens within their practice. What I mean by that is recently we shared an email campaign with an owner and we ran it and they ended up getting a ton of leads, like 70. They didn't follow up at all and they didn't convert any of those leads... so that is a pretty big problem.

The willingness to take responsibility for what is happening within the four walls of your private practice is really, really big.

That is who this is for.

Again, my purpose for you is as I am sharing this book and as you are reading about my experiences and as I am telling you about these successful systems that I have implemented... that I will give you opportunities to learn more... to dive deeper into that topic..

Because in print we are very much limited to a couple of pages on those ideas, it is pretty limited, but I can tell you that I do have a lot of other information.

Wherever it is appropriate in the book, I will give you a resource where you can go and learn more about exactly what I am doing.

My first purpose, and this is full-disclosure, is that I am sharing information with other private practice owners and frankly I know that most of those owners that fit the five things that I am looking for are probably going to go on and do other stuff with us through Breakthrough PT Marketing.

Realize that this is the primary purpose of this book.

The second thing, the purpose that I want to give you is a sense of control over your own destiny... knowing that you can control your marketing, that you can switch from a model of being reliant primarily on physician referrals and switch that over to primarily Direct Access, where you are getting more and more patients every month from your past patient base and also the general public.

The book is really about me sharing that and I want to give you a big shortcut so that you don't have to go through the same exact losses that I went through.

As you go through, if you have a question on anything, you can always email me. The best way to reach me is **chad@breakthroughptmarketing.com.**

Let's get started.

Chapter 2

Picture Your Perfect Practice

"We become what we think about."
- Earl Nightingale

Earl Nightingale in his famous recording, The Strangest Secret in 1954, revealed that the strangest secret is "We become what we think about."

The purpose of this exercise that we are about to go through is to clearly define what you want your life, your private practice, your body, and your relationships....and what you want it to look like.

If we don't go through this exercise, what happens is we become like a rudderless ship with no direction at all...

So in order for you to achieve what you want to achieve in your private practice, you have to define what that looks like, what the destination looks like.

Personally, for me, from experience, I really struggled my first 2 years in private practice...

I knew that where I was at then, let's call that "Point A," was not where I ultimately wanted to be.

But I never really defined what the destination was.

I never really defined what "Point B" looked like.

I never really defined what my perfect practice looked like or what I was trying to work toward.

So again, I really struggled for 2 years... and then somebody walked me through this exercise.

They just started asking me questions about Point B.

We are going to go through that in a second, but first, I want to share with you what the biggest barrier to you achieving your perfect practice...

Self-Limiting Beliefs

Self-limiting beliefs are the biggest barrier between where you are at now and where you want to be in your private practice life.

What are self-limiting beliefs?

They are things that we say—that inner voice in our head—that change our action and limit our action.

So if we go back to The Strangest Secret, which is "We become what we think about," the private practice owner who is really struggling will say things like...

"Well, I can't grow my practice because the hospital systems own all of the referral sources in my area."

So they block themselves from a solution because they have just told their subconscious mind, "I can't grow my practice."

They will be blind to solutions...ignore the solutions that could work.

Other self-limiting beliefs include:

"The reason I can't grow my practice is the POPTS practice down the street."

"Reimbursements are declining."

"With insurance companies, it seems like we have to do more and more work for less and less money."

"I have never done anything successful in my life."

"I have always failed. I'm a failure."

"I can't be successful."

"The healthcare environment is not the best."

"My staff is wrong."

"My billing is wrong."

"My location is wrong."

"I need physician referrals to live."

These are all self-limiting beliefs - all little recordings that we tell ourselves that stop us from seeing the solution.

Remember Before You Opened Up? The Entrepreneurial Journey

Most of us, before we started into private practice, said, "Here is how I want to leave my stamp on the world. Here is how I want to leave my impact."

Most of us had a jaded experience and then we set out to start a private practice that embodied our belief system.

When we go out and we have our first loss—maybe we have trouble making a payday, maybe things aren't turning out financially as well as we thought, maybe we lost a referral source—we usually go through that...so to jump from impact to the next phase requires some sort of loss.

We all go through that.
We all experience that.
Most of us get to a point where we begin compromising...

We say, "Well, if I just made enough money, then it would be worth it."

I know for me, after I experienced that first loss... within 6 months of opening my private practice, I lost my top referral source that moved out of state... my compromise became, "If I just made double the income that I would make working for somebody else, I'm willing to do this."

I ended up working 75 hours a week to replace my wife's income.

That was what I settled for because that was my destination.

Then eventually, most of us progress and mature to the point in our private practice lives where we say, "Now I want to be able to make X amount of dollars. I want to make this much money, make the same amount of money but I don't want to work 75 hours a week. If I just work 40 or even 50 hours, it would be better than what I am doing now."

So we progress from impact... to a money goal... to a time goal.

Then eventually, for those of us that solve that problem of the time goal, we then move back to the impact... which is, "Ok, here is how I'm going to leave my stamp on the world."

Self-limiting beliefs prevent us from doing that...or at least make the journey take longer.

As we go through this exercise, which we are about to get started here in a second, Picturing Your Perfect Practice, I just want to take away all of those beliefs...or suspend them for a minute.

And I want you to go through this exercise without any limitations at all.

Don't worry where you are at right now for the sake of the exercise, picture where you want to be without any limits.

Image if you just had a magic wand and you could wave that magic wand and instantly have what you name.

What would that look like in your private practice?

The 1st Section that we are going to look at is People...

So for you:

1. How many hours are you treating in your perfect practice?
2. How many total hours are you working per week?
3. Will this give you enough time to invest with your family?
4. Will this give you enough time to invest in your health? Your interests?
5. Would you be better rested, less stressed and healthier if this was your work schedule?

Your team or staff:

1. Does your staff bring problems to you or do they bring you solutions?
2. Do you carry their problems home with you?
3. Can you take off for 30 days and not worry that your business is running smoothly?
4. Is your staff well trained?
5. Are they well paid and incentivized?
6. Do you have a waiting list of candidates applying, even though you are not advertising a position? (Remember, this is your ideal practice...)
7. Does each staff member know his/her responsibility and what they are accountable for?
8. Would you hire everyone on your team again?
9. Do they add to your energy or do they take it away?

Your practice:

1. How big is your practice?
2. How many locations do you have?
3. What do you specialize in? What are you known for?

The 2nd Section is on Money...

1. How much money are you making in your perfect practice? (Consider both total clinic income and profitability.)
2. Are you maxing out your 401K, your 529 contributions (college funds for your kids), and your savings for the future? And are you out of debt with this plan?
3. Can you do everything you want to do if you are making this much money?

The 3rd Section is Marketing...

1. Do you have systems in place to consistently get referrals from the big 3 target markets?
2. Are you scientific with your marketing to maximize return on investment?
3. Are you consistently attracting patients who don't complain about time, money or distance?
4. Do you know how to control your marketing and plan ahead for any slow seasons?
5. Do you know how to attract Direct Access patients?

Now... take your answers from above and write out, in present tense, the picture of your perfect practice.

("For example, I'm treating 20 hours per week and I work a total of 40 hours per week. I'm home for dinner every night with my wife and kids. I take weekends off and spend it with my family. I am healthy and have time to take care of my own health, exercising 5 days per week. I am calm and at peace and have a healthy life.")

So go through this and write out in present tense what your perfect practice looks like.

Other variables that you may want to consider and include:

1. Do you own the building that your private practice is in?
2. With your marketing systems in place, do you know how to attract Physical Therapists?
3. Can you attract the type of patients that you want to treat?
4. Do these patients value and respect your knowledge, your time and your expertise?
5. Do you feel like you are constantly going out and reinventing the marketing wheel?
6. Are you doing cash pay? Are you attracting affluent patients who can overcome time, distance and money and aren't dropping off because of co-pay issues or otherwise?

Personnel we already covered.

When we were at the private practice conference, there was another practice owner who came up to me and spoke and said, "The reason I love these events is because I just want to look my competition in the eye and know that I am whipping their butt." (For the record...not my goal).

Perhaps that is not your goal, but do you have a goal of what you are really trying to achieve and have you written that out?

7. Are you involved in the community? Are you leaving an impact? Are you invested in goodwill causes?
8. Do you have authority, celebrity, and expertise within your community?

9. Are you known for something and known for it well? Are you the PT for back pain and sciatica? Are you the vestibular specialist? Are you the Therapist that is amazing with shoulders or ankles or CrossFit injuries?
10. Are you or your practice considered innovative? Full of ideas? OR are you just the status quo?
11. Are you truly the first choice for the people in your community who you want to attract, especially when they consider medications, injections or surgery?
12. Are you respected for your expertise?
13. Within your private practice, do you have a handle on your metrics? Are you in control? Are you growing?
14. Are you goal-oriented?
15. Are you having fun? Or are you stressed?
16. Do you have new equipment or do you have run-down, ill-maintained equipment in your perfect practice?
17. Is your facility clean?
18. Do you have a full marketing funnel built out (which we will talk about in a later chapter), with a soft landing to your physical therapy services and a profitable back-end in place?

Throughout the Picturing Your Perfect Practice exercise, you want to consider these variables. Take a look at your overall practice and be as defined as possible.

Again, consider these variables.

Write out your answers to these questions.

And then, create a statement in present tense about exactly what your perfect practice looks like.

Remember... it doesn't really matter if you believe this is possible or not right now.

I have seen practice owners that wrote down what they thought was impossible at the time, and they have gone on to achieve that much faster than they ever thought possible.

When I first went through this exercise, I wrote down something that I thought I would never achieve.

Just because I was told that there were no boundaries, I went for it.

Oddly enough... I ended up achieving that in less than 12 months.

You can do that same exact thing.

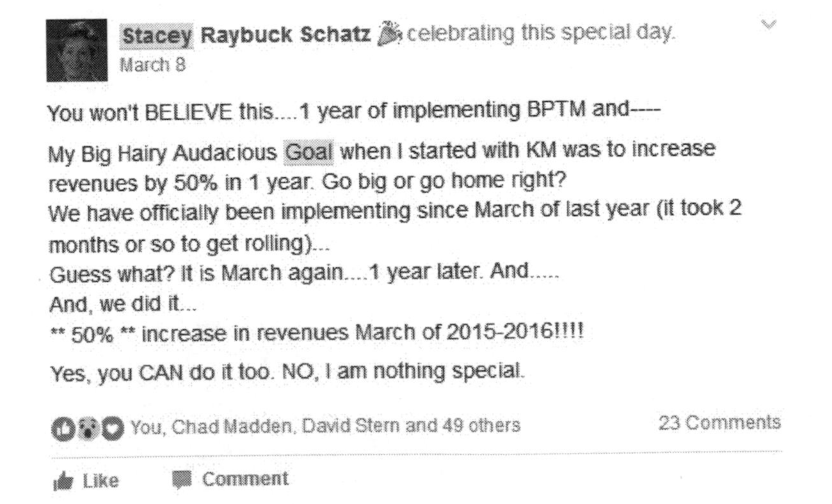

Chapter 3

The 5 Trends That Are Shaping Private Practice Physical Therapy Today

---

How the Healthcare Landscape Has Changed Over the Past 15 Years And What You Can Do About It.

In this chapter, I'm going to review 5 trends that shape the way that successful private practice Physical Therapists operate today... 4 of them seem troubling on the surface and 1 of them is positive...but only if used the right way.

The first area that we are going to look at is a POPTS practice - that stands for Physician-Owned Physical Therapy Services.

The following is taken from the website www.AAOS.org, the American Academy of Orthopedic Surgeons.

This is their statement on Physician-Owned Physical Therapy:

" Physical Therapy has long been an integral part of the scope of services provided by Orthopedic Surgeons. In fact, the Physical Therapy profession arose from the initiatives of Orthopedists who recognized the need for individuals with skills in exercise and rehabilitation to maximize patient recovery and rehabilitation. Physician-Owned Physical Therapy Services (POPTS) foster a cohesive team approach to care, which translates to accessible high-quality treatment centered around the needs and best interest of the patient. Despite the distinct benefits that having the choice to use in-office physical therapy provides to patients, National Physical Therapist groups continue to spearhead a strategic and aggressive campaign in an effort to prohibit or limit POPTS. These attempts also impact Physical Therapists who should have the freedom to seek employment as they choose (whether with a physician or not), and not have their career choices restrained by unnecessary government intervention. Even physicians who do not employ Physical Therapists or have an ownership interest in a Physical Therapy service should see this as a critical issue - one that encroaches on the ability of Orthopedic Surgeons to deliver the best care possible, and limits patient access and choice. The AAOS believes that patients should have access to quality comprehensive and non-fragmented care. Doctors, Nurses, Physician's Assistants, Physical Therapists and other health practitioners work together, often in the same office, to provide comprehensive care to patients. Separation of these services would only serve to disrupt the patient's treatment and farther inconvenience them. The AAOS also believes that Physician-Owned Physical Therapy Services should continue to be an alternative for patients. The patient should be given the ability to choose the site of care.

Physicians employing Physical Therapists should communicate to the patient their financial interest in any Physical Therapy practice prior to referring the patient to the site. The Physician should also discuss possible alternate sites for Physical Therapy services. In all instances, the AAOS believes that the best interest of the patient should be foremost when referring a patient for Physical Therapy services. ”

This is the statement of the American Academy of Orthopedic Surgeons on POPTS practices.

From my own experience of working in a POPTS practice for 2 years, I can tell you this:

Communication between the Orthopedic Surgeon and the Physical Therapist is no different in an independent versus a POPTS clinic based on my observation from a Physical Therapist perspective.

The troubling issue that I had working for a POPTS practice is that regardless of what I did as a Physical Therapist and the quality of care that I provided, the referrals continued to come.

So if I had a co-worker who was providing the best possible plan of care, world-class care and outcomes, and I decided to slack in any way at all, my schedule continued to be full and so did hers as well.

As we know, in independent private practice physical therapy... that is not an option.

All care must be at optimal level... otherwise, we will lose the trust of the patients and physicians alike - and ultimately be out of business and have to close our doors.

POPTS practices are a real obstacle and barrier to the survival of private practice physical therapy, and if we don't recognize that, it is going to be impossible to survive long term...

More on how to handle this in a minute.

The second trend is hospital systems.

Over the past 15 years, there has been a lot of pressure on hospital systems to continue to generate profits, especially with declining reimbursements and increased paperwork required within the present healthcare environment.

One of the strategies that a majority of the healthcare systems in the country has taken on is to purchase, first, family physicians and more importantly employ those family physicians to make referrals within the hospital system to ancillary services.

(At least in my area, Central Pennsylvania, it began with family physicians...)

More than 70% of all referral sources in my immediate area surrounding my physical therapy private practice are now employed within one of 3 hospital systems.

The hospital systems have now moved on to employing specialists and urgent care physicians.

The one exception (as of today when I am writing this book) is Orthopedic Surgeons.

All of the Orthopedic Surgeons in my area are presently independent... although they certainly have surgical rights in the hospitals; they are NOT required or policed to send their PT patients to the hospital systems.

Unfortunately, 100% of the Orthopedic Surgeons in our area are affiliated with a POPTS Physical Therapy practice.

The other troubling issue with hospital systems is that not only do they prevent referrals of patients outside of the hospital system, but they also frequently enjoy a stronger or better reimbursement than the independent private practice Physical Therapist. (At worst...this is supported by one specific case I've seen with an actual EOB - Explanation of Benefits - for a PT session within the hospital.)

At least in my area, as I have heard other private practice owners talk as well and share similar experiences all over the US, many hospital systems restrict their employed physicians from even speaking with independent Physical Therapists.

They block the communication.

This is absolutely a problem and a barrier for the private practice Physical Therapist.

The third trend is insurance companies.

Over the last 15 years, seemingly, reimbursements have declined and paperwork has increased. So it has become more and more difficult to get reimbursed for our services.

One of the most troubling aspects of insurance companies, because many of us as a private practice owner are not only a provider, we are also a consumer... we are the purchaser of health insurance from the health insurance companies to provide to our staff, our employees.

Presently, 100% of insurance companies in my immediate area offer some commercial advertisement representation of providing higher quality of care to the consumer and some aspect of wellness and healthier living.

Unfortunately, for those of us in private practice PT, over the last 15 years, consumers have been hit with progressively higher co-pays...almost discouraging conservative care, health and wellness.

When I first got out of school, I can remember a patient complaining that her co-pay had gone from $5 to $10 over the course of the last year and that that blocked her from coming to every visit (she was a post-op patient).

Unfortunately... that trend has continued.

It is no longer a $5 or $10 co-pay (that is unheard of)...it is a $40 or $50 co-pay, which tends to be higher than the PCP (Primary Care Physician) visit.

Also, many patients no longer have a co-pay at all because they are dealing with a $1,500 to $3,000 annual deductibles, where they are basically paying cash for their physical therapy care.

The question remains... if insurance companies truly wanted to provide health and wellness services and an emphasis on conservative care, why not reward patients who opt for conservative care first? ...and don't opt for medications, injections and surgery and more invasive procedures that are more expensive to the healthcare system and ultimately result in lower health outcomes and wellness?

The other troubling aspect, at least that we have experienced here in private practice, is that of "tiering."

Tiering is when an insurance company or an outside review company places the given providers in an area in different tiers or different levels.

Depending on the tier that one is placed in, it also determines the access to care for patients that seek out that provider.

For example, in our area, a provider that is in Tier A enjoys very little paperwork for authorization of care.

Somebody who is in Tier B must go through significantly more paperwork for an authorization.

A Provider in Tier C ultimately has to get just about every 4 visits authorized for physical therapy care.

The issue with many of the review companies in the tiering model is that frequently what those of us in private practice PT are compared to is the national average for visits per diagnosis.

One of the things that I have heard is, "if I can get a patient better in 6.7 visits and it takes you 8.3 that that somehow correlates to better or a higher quality of care."

Unfortunately, this is not the issue as it doesn't include a focus on the most important variable... which is OUTCOMES.

Nor does it focus on a patient's compliance to care.

So if I am a Physical Therapist and I have driven patients away and I am a "Discharge Machine" and patients tend not to complete their plans of care with me, I may have a super low average visit per plan of care.

Does this necessarily mean that I should be placed in a higher tier with easier access to authorization for patients that I see because I am a lousy, underperforming Physical Therapist?

I would hope not.

Unfortunately, the present situation does not reflect that.

The fourth trend is corporate physical therapy.

Within 13 miles of my office in Harrisburg, Pennsylvania is the headquarters of the largest rehab provider in the country - that now owns and operates over 30 clinics that I compete with directly in my immediate market.

There is a second physical therapy company that is a Top 10 company nationally with regards to size... they are headquartered less than 6 miles away.

The simple fact is that corporate physical therapy companies can enjoy greater marketing spend and tend to focus on branding versus those of us in private practice.

What becomes the advantage for the larger companies can also become a disadvantage for them as well because they tend to not use direct response marketing, which is much easier for us to employ and which I will be sharing with you throughout the pages of this book.

They also tend to operate more slowly, so if something needs to get done, the layers of management often cannot react in time or as quickly as compared to the private practice physical therapy owner.

So we have to look at what advantages the corporate giants employ and how we can win in a competitive market based on what they seem to have as strengths... which also may be their weaknesses.

We want to focus and win the competition in areas that we have the advantage.

The fifth is the one possible positive trend that has happened in private practice physical therapy in the last 15 years... and that is Direct Access.

As of right now, in present day, as this book was written... on the American Physical Therapy Association website, 49 of the 50 states within the United States now have Direct Access to care in some form or another.

The issue is that Direct Access is a destination for Physical Therapists.

That is something that we want.

It is part of the APTA's Vision 2020.

However, Direct Access is not a destination for consumers. It is not what they need and want unless it is positioned in the right way.

The one mistake that I will frequently see private practice owners make is when they are advertising that they are Direct Access licensed, that they say just that... that they have Direct Access.

Unfortunately, this means nothing to the patient.

The patient's typical question is this, "Do I need to see my doctor first?"

The common answer is, "No, unless you are a Medicare subscriber or recipient."

At least that is what the question is in my area or one of the obscure smaller private insurance companies that requires a referral.

Fortunately, there are significantly less private insurance companies that now require that somebody get a referral for physical therapy prior to being seen by a Physical Therapist. More on advertising "Direct Access" as a mistake...

The reason that this is typically delivered as a mistake is that Direct Access is not a button.

It is not a reason that somebody would seek help from a Physical Therapist. There are other lead magnet benefits...there are other needs and wants of the patient prior to Direct Access even entering into the discussion.

So, Direct Access should not be used in the beginning of a conversation.

It should be used at the end...and only to cover a small hurdle, "Do I need to see my doctor first?"

Having said that...15 years ago, private practice physical therapy was all about getting referrals from physicians.

Based on the trends of today with POPTS practices, hospital systems, insurance companies, corporate physical therapy companies and Direct Access, we are now entering into this new phase of healthcare... which is the consumer-driven market.

Consumers are more educated than ever before about their condition when they are coming in for care.

Fewer and fewer patients that we are seeing in our private practice are saying, "I'm here because my doctor sent me."

While Direct Access was a destination for Physical Therapists, what many of us continued to do in private practice was continue to use branding to advertise for Direct Access.

Fortunately, in a consumer-driven market, there is a method of marketing that wins every single time.

That is **DIRECT RESPONSE MARKETING.**

We are going to talk about direct response marketing here in the remainder of the book and how you can implement the principles and concepts of it in your private practice.

Basically, you can also think of direct response marketing as content marketing - that is delivering a valuable message that is needed and wanted by the consumer so that they raise their hand and say, "Yes, I have back pain and I want help and want to learn more from you."

There are multiple ways to do this and in the pages ahead, we will explore a few of the most popular ways to do this.

In summary, there are 4 seemingly troubling trends that are shaping private practice physical therapy today and 1 positive one.

However, all 5 of these trends...when harnessed the right way...can be a huge advantage for the private practice Physical Therapist.

The way that we win this and that we succeed is NOT by saying how unfair things are, by saying that POPTS practices aren't fair and that we need to fight against that... or that hospital systems aren't fair and we need to fight that...insurance companies are being ridiculous and fighting that...or corporate physical therapy companies are "Walmart-ing" us or "Amazon-ing" us or making fun of those entities.

The way that we win in Private Practice is by controlling what we can control and by realizing that rules have changed in the healthcare environment not only today, but also for the future.

Chapter 4

The #1 Single Most Important Question You Need to Know About Your Private Practice and Its Survival – The Crucial Question

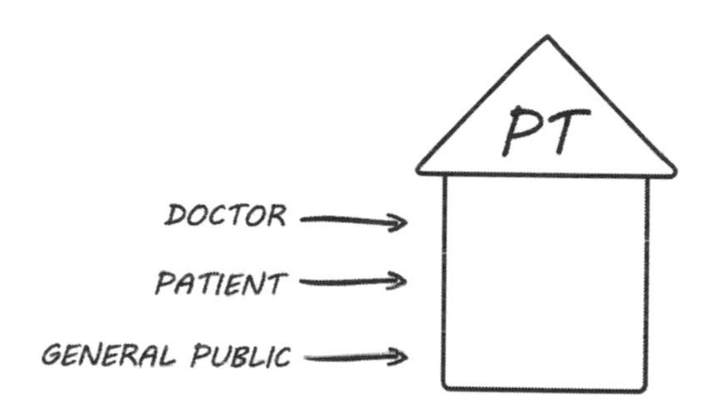

Think about the last 12 months of your private practice and the new patients that you have seen...

You can basically attract new patients from 3 different target markets:

Target market #1 is referrals from **Physicians** and referral sources.

Target market #2 is your past and present **Patients** - either returning for additional care or referring other people to you.

Target market #3 is Direct Access from the general **Public**. So this might be somebody who comes to your workshop or who reads your book and comes in without a physician referral and without a referral from a past patient. So strictly a Direct Access patient.

Consider the last 12 months and what percentage do each of the above 3 represent for your Private Practice?

What percentage of your New Patients came from **Physicians**?
What percentage of your New Patients came from **Patients**?
What percentage of your New Patients came from the **Public**?

Just by going through this exercise, most practice owners realize that they likely have a very high percentage of their referrals coming from physicians.

With the trends that we already covered...which are hospitals buying physician practices and employing physicians and also POPTS practices... you can see that those private practices that are relying more than 50% of their practice on physician referrals may be in trouble.

(And many practice owners have found out already that they are in trouble.)

The key question is, *"How do we shift a physical therapy private practice referral percentage from being primarily physician referrals to that of being more balanced?"*...where maybe we have 1/3 coming from physicians and referral sources plus 1/3 coming from past patients returning for additional care and referrals from those past patients plus 1/3 from the general public and Direct Access.

So where are you at? And where do you want to be?

Why is this important?

If you walked into one of your exam rooms and a patient was sitting on the table for their 97001, their initial examination, and you asked them, "Hey, how did you end up here at XYZ Physical Therapy?"

Option A, the patient says, "I'm here because my doctor sent me here."

And Option B is, "I'm here because I read your book...I came to your workshop...I watched a video of you and I want you to treat me."

So percentage-wise... the patient in Option A, what do you think the likelihood is that they complete their plan of care and that they actually graduate from physical therapy?

Just from experience, I can tell you this is about 50%.

What do you think the chances are that patient B completes their plan of care and graduates and achieves their goals?

It is 90%.

Just from experience, if you have been in private practice for a while or simply if you have been a Physical Therapist for a while, you can see that we want as many Option B's as possible. Because what happens over time is IF we have a private practice that is relying on physician referrals, only about half of their patient base is going to be responsive to future promotions and marketing efforts.

Let's face it... people who don't graduate physical therapy...people who don't meet their goals are very unlikely to return in the future.

They have a jaded experience with PT. They don't think it can work for them and they are highly unlikely to return in the future...even if their physician writes another script for PT.

I'm not saying it never happens (patients returning to PT after a failed PT experience)...I'm saying that the likelihood of it happening is not high.

However, if we have a physical therapy practice where the majority of the patients are coming in via Direct Access from the general public or past patients returning and that percentage is higher than let's say 50% of the total new patients in that practice, what will happen over time is a larger percentage of that practice's past population base is more likely to respond and return for additional care, for additional services which we will talk about here a little bit later how to do that.

The big point that I want to make here is that people who come see us or come see you because they consume your content...

They read a blog or a report or a book that you have out...

They see you on video...

Or they come to one of your live workshops or have seen one of your workshop recordings...

THAT is truly Content Marketing.

So you are putting out content that establishes you as an Authority, a Celebrity, and as an Expert in whatever your given niche of physical therapy is. (This is referred to as A.C.E...more on this in a bit).

So with the physician in content marketing, the problem is that most doctors don't have any training at all in physical therapy. Most often, they have very little PT experience...resulting in a shallow reality of what PT can do.

One Physician's Perspective on PT

One of my favorite stories to demonstrate this was with an Orthopedic Surgeon who approached me shortly after I opened my private practice.

He and his partner took me out to lunch and right away in the conversation I could figure that they had an angle, that they had a reason for taking me out to lunch. And it was they wanted me to come run their physical therapy practice, their POPTS practice.

Well, I was already leasing space. I was already established in private practice seeing 100 to 120 visits a week...

I didn't want to give that up. I didn't want to give up my lease to go run their private practice. That wouldn't really make sense.

The key point of that story is during the conversation, I asked the one Orthopedic Surgeon, "Have you ever been down in your own physical therapy practice?"

He sheepishly admitted that he had never stepped foot in his own POPTS practice. He had no familiarity at all and really didn't understand my perspective that a good Physical Therapist...whoever he decided to hire (because it wasn't going to be me)...is essentially protecting him and his surgical outcomes.

He really didn't understand this.

He had no reality, no perspective, no understanding at all of how important physical therapy was. I don't think this is the exception...it seems to me to be extremely common.

Most referral sources, if you ask them the amount of exposure to physical therapy and conservative care during their training, during their residencies... it is usually very limited or next to zero.

Lead Magnets and the General Public

With the general public, if somebody is in your area and they have never experienced your physical therapy before...they don't know you.

However, if they consume your content... you quickly have positioned yourself with Authority, Celebrity and Expertise and they are much more likely to respond.

The one thing that we are going to talk about with content marketing later in Killer Marketing Secrets is something called a **"Lead Magnet"**.

Your options here are a report, a book, a blog post - which perhaps you post via Facebook or some other sort of social media. It could be a workshop, it could be a video, it could be some other sort of content...

You are sharing valuable information (usually for free), usually with minimal commitment from the consumer...other than possibly an ability to have an ongoing conversation with the person who consumes the Lead Magnet.

What you are looking for...if you are thinking about a Lead Magnet...you are looking for people in the general public to raise their hand and say, *"Yes, I have back pain every time I stand and walk. Yes, I have shoulder pain. Yes, I have neck pain. Yes, I have a knee problem. Yes, I have a hip problem. Yes, I want to keep running and my doctor told me that I can't run anymore."*

Or something similar...

You want those people to raise their hand and then you want to offer them valuable content that truly helps them.

<u>One other secret here is that readers and people who consume content are much better patients.</u>

If you only get 140 characters on Twitter to convey your message, it is much less effective than somebody who sits and reads your 80 page book on back pain... or attends your 1 hour webinar on back pain and sciatica...

People who consume more content make better patients. They have bought more into the process and they will respect you more for your expertise.

Most owners that I talk with very much want to shift from relying on physician referrals and thinking and saying, *"I need physician referrals to stay in business."*

Many want to shift and get themselves in a position where they are no longer having to rely on physician referrals for the viability and the profitability of their practice.

So let's move on and talk about that...

Want to Learn How I Pivoted My Private Practice from 95% Physician Referrals to 80% Direct Access While Doubling Profitability?

Join me on the POPTS Killer Webinar and Learn:

- How We Attract 40 New Patient Each Month Who Have a POPTS Physician as Their Primary Doctor...
- How We Attract Over 1,000 Direct Access Patients Each Year...
- Learn **direct access** marketing strategies that are working in private practice TODAY and **STOP relying on physician referrals.**
- The 3-step process to building marketing systems that deliver patients every month, automatically.

- Learn how to position yourself with patients and physicians to maximize your referrals where most PTs have given up.
- Practice Owner reveals how he grew 600% in 30 months AND doubled profits last year in spite of hospitals owning 65% of local family physicians, 100% of all orthopedic specialists working in one of two groups with their own POPTS practices AND being less than 13 miles from the Corporate Headquarters of 2 of the largest PT companies in the US.
- **BONUS** - You'll get a chance to attend a live Implementation Bootcamp to implement direct access marketing systems with me, in person, for FREE.

Register for the POPTS Killer Webinar at:
www.POPTSKiller.com

Chapter 5

The Four Levels of Private Practice PT Owners

Hall Of Famer
All-Star
Major Leaguer
Minor Leaguer

Back in Chapter 2, we talked about the idea of your Dream Practice.

The scenario that most of us are in as private practice owners is that we want to go from Point A to Point B... and Point B is our Dream Practice.

Again, back in Chapter 2, we have defined exactly what that looks like for you...(if you haven't completed that exercise...invest an hour in your future and go back and do that exercise now)...

However, another important part is we need to define where you are at right now.

So when I am talking with owners anywhere in the US and abroad, the thing that I will often hear is, *"I want to take my practice to the next level."*

Well, in order to do that, we need to know:

1. The level that you are at right now AND
2. What the levels of private practice PT are...

So let's get started with #2.

The Minor Leaguer

The Minor Leaguer is just happy to be in the game. They are happy to be a rookie. They are happy to be a practice owner.

Who is this? This is the new private practice owner who is just starting out. Their M.O. (or their modus operandi) is unconscious incompetence.

What that means is they have no idea...not a clue...they don't even know what they don't know yet.

They may have self-limiting beliefs such as: *"I need to rely on physician referrals" or "I need referrals to stay in business"...* but they don't yet havethe experience of failure to know that they have limitations. They just took the leap from being an employee...Staff Physical Therapist...Manager... Clinical Director to being an Owner.

Their common thought is, *"I'm my own boss now."*

You know how it is...most of us have had that jaded experience working for somebody else. That jadedness is what prompted us to go work for ourselves by becoming a Private Practice Owner.

The Minor Leaguer is likely focused on the "Owner" title or "CEO" of one or a few employees.

They will also focus on the logo, the slogan, business cards, website, letterhead and likely an informative tri-fold brochure about their "high-quality of care".

They are usually proud that their name is within the name of the business... or the originality and cleverness of their PT business name.

They may think that success in private practice is luck or pure chance.

They know that they need marketing and the new patients that it produces to survive, but they aren't aware of more than one or two ways of attracting new patients.

They have no systems in place and they are not even thinking about systems.

If you are a Minor Leaguer, **YOU are your business.**

Oddly enough, you are still trading time for money. So when you were working for somebody else as an employee, you were trading time for money. Right now, because you are your business, you are still trading time for money.

Most Minor Leaguers will view hiring other employees as an expense.

We will get into this in a later Chapter, how this thought is an error.

Usually their confidence is really high...especially in the beginning.

They haven't really been slapped yet. They haven't had a loss yet. So this swiftly becomes "overwhelm" once slapped.

They may have a handful of employees.

The common thought is *"If I could just make a little more money..."*

Or *"If I could just make X amount of dollars...everything will be OK."*

They have no personnel control.

Their thoughts on marketing are usually along the lines of certifications or the type of PT services that they offer or that education should suffice.

"I'm a DPT or I have Direct Access or the OCS and patients will flock to me."

The other thing that they will often say...

And this is funny because the MO, modus operandi, is unconscious incompetence... So they don't know what they don't know yet.

They will frequently say, *"I know. I know. I know."*

They will have that recording and that saying just repeating in their head over and over and over again and it blocks them from learning.

They often mistake recognition for knowledge and understanding.

If I go back to when I first opened my private practice, this is exactly what I was going through...

I thought that if I went out and got certifications or specialized education and began practicing in a niche area of physical therapy, that patients would flock to me.

I quickly found out that was not the case.

I also went through that "feeling of overwhelm" because I knew that my business relied on marketing and the new patients that it attracted.

But I had no idea how to do that.

I quickly realized that the assumptions that I had made were way off...and not grounded in reality...

MINOR LEAGUER

1. *They ARE their business*
2. *Marked by one or no established, tested marketing pathways.*
3. *They are focused on their own certifications, clinical education and being an owner.*
4. *M.O. - "Unconscious Incompetence."*
5. *They say things like, "If I could just make a little more money"*
6. *In the beginning they are overly confident, then after a loss, they become overwhelmed.*
7. *They usually have no reserves and they are compiling debt.*

The Major Leaguer

Who is the Major Leaguer?

The Major Leaguer is making good money, often very good money...by working 2 full-time jobs.

They are still trading time for money and the way that they are running right now is not sustainable.

Their M.O. is **conscious incompetence.**

(This is a level up from unconscious incompetence that we saw in the Minor Leaguer.)

They are aware of systems and that they should have them, but they have no knowledge or inadequate knowledge of how to implement them.

They perceive they do know what to do... even though they don't know how to implement.

Like the Minor Leaguer, they mistake recognition for understanding and knowledge... just now with greater ability...this makes them a little more dangerous.

They have had some losses.

Maybe they have lost their top referral source or they wasted money on a marketing method that didn't pay off as planned.

They have been pressed to make payroll once or twice and may have even suffered a financial loss.

The big thing that they are marked by here is **fear of future losses.** They are angry at their situation.

When the Major League owner is there in the practice, everything is growing. But they hold everything together. They are the glue. Everything crashes without them...vacations or taking time off are nearly impossible.

Personnel? They may now have 8-10 or even a dozen employees.

The Major League owner subconsciously undermines them and doesn't know how to empower their staff.

Occasionally the Major League Owner will answer his own phone, do his own scheduling, collect his co-pays, or do his own laundry and cleaning. They are not trying to work themselves out of a job yet and they don't know how.

The Major League Owner manages everything.

The staff brings every problem to the owner.

The things they commonly say are:

"If I could just have more time."

"If I could just work a normal 40 hour week and make the same money or maybe even a little bit less, then I could have more time to invest with my ... . (fill in the blank with family, spouse, personal interest, other business interest, etc.)"

"If I could just go learn more about systems, but I don't have time."

They are usually critical of others. So they are usually critical of POPTS practices, hospital systems, large competing PT companies.

They are usually heavily invested in big time excuses.

They have high levels of stress.

The Crab in the Pot...

They will often feel like the crab in the pot.

You know the analogy - if you are steaming crabs, inevitably one will reach up to the edge of the pot and begin to pull itself out and all of the other crabs will reach up to that crab and pull it back in. They often suffer that crab-in-the-pot syndrome where they pull others down in an effort to "help them."

They are the "middle class" of private practice owners.

They have been burnt and now they feel jaded and often angry.

There is a fear of loss, especially a fear of future financial loss.

So they batten down the hatches. Take no chances...don't want to do anything. Do the status quo. No risk at all.

They put out fires constantly and their practice is seemingly always in rocky waters.

The owner is the problem solver.

If you are a Major League Owner, that person...the problem solver...is you. They chase referrals and patients. They don't know how to magnetically attract them. They view 'limited referrals to go around' in any given area.

I have hit upon this quite a few times where a person will think that there are only 100 patients that possibly get referred out in a week. That is all that there are in their area, even though there are 100,000 people living there.

They view that there are only a limited number of patients in any geographic area. They live with a viewpoint of scarcity.

They will often have self-limiting beliefs such as, "I know. I know. I know."

But they haven't done yet. So they have the knowledge but they don't have the doing.

MAJOR LEAGUER

1. Believes there are a limited number of referral sources in any geographical area and they end up **chasing referrals.**
2. M.O. - "Conscious Incompetence."
3. They will say things like, **"If I just had more time."**
4. They have **fear of future losses,** then they become angry and jaded.
5. They are usually a **high income earner with little or no equity.**

The All-Star

Who is this? This is the owner who has his/her stuff together.

The MO is **conscious competence.**

The All-Star Owner has good staff. They receive compliments routinely on how they run their practice or their business.

They have made the choice of how many hours they treat. So if they want to treat 40 hours a week, they treat 40 hours a week. If they want to treat 15 hours a week, they treat 15 hours a week. If they don't want to treat at all, they have done that as well.

They have leaders or managers in place who run their systems.

What this does is it allows the All-Star Owner to focus on creating more business...serving more people and a greater need.

Commonly what will happen in this (especially when the owner makes a jump from Major League to All-Star)...they may start to not know what to do with themselves.

They will say things like, *"Now what?"*

They have marketing systems in place that attract patients steadily.

They have multiple systems in place for reception area, scheduling, billing, treating, finances, and marketing.

There is a systematic effort to give each patient a great experience or even a world-class experience.

The All-Star Owner has a consistent effort to learn and improve upon their systems and freely exchanges with other practice owners.

They have a solid network of other successful All-Star Owners. (They tend to know each other.)

An All-Star Owner no longer believes they know everything. They don't even say it and they don't act like it.

The business is profitable and viable.

They have adequate financial reserves to fall back on in case of any emergencies and the practice can handle just about any healthcare crisis.

There is little or no debt.

The All-Star Owner is not concerned about their kid's tuition costs, the price of the safest SUV for their family or that the price of a Disney vacation for their family has doubled in the last 3 years.

Their staff is well paid and responsible and trustworthy.

The practice owner may even be newsworthy and earn free press in the local newspaper, TV station or even earn recognition from a PT journal.

The private practice is admired by other PTs.

With regards to marketing, the All-Star owner has a large, growing, loyal patient base and could weather any referral source drop-off or change.

The referral base is wide with no doctor representing more than 5% of the total referral base.

They have multiple successful marketing pathways in place to attract ideal clients who are compliant patients who seek care and are willing and able to pay.

They may have multiple clinics or one large clinic.

The All-Star Owner and their team feel like they can solve any problem. To do that, they have built a steady training system of books, coaching, experts in courses, etc. to consistently improve.

They have a healthy curiosity.

The All-Star Owner is a true business owner.

ALL-STAR

1. True business owner
2. Has multiple established marketing systems in place and those systems are tested.
3. M.O. - "Conscious Competence."
4. They usually say, "Now what?"
5. They have a healthy curiosity then possibly boredom, if there's not a New, Bigger Game.
6. They have usually no debt and adequate cash reserves.
7. They can afford affluence.
8. They are not worried about money and they have systems for finances, personnel & marketing.

The Hall of Famer

Who is the Hall of Famer?

This is the private practice owner who is establishing a legacy through advocacy, teaching and being a shining beacon in the community of private practice physical therapy owners.

The M.O. is **unconscious competence.**

"Success in private practice" is now second nature to the Hall of Fame Owner.

The language of success and the act of creating solutions is so ingrained in the Hall of Famer's subconscious mind that he/she occasionally forgets that all other private practice owners are not on the same level.

The Hall of Famer has met or is actively meeting all of his business goals, personal goals, financial goals, time goals, etc. and has produced a balanced life full of amazing experiences and memories.

It is possible that the Hall of Fame Owner has sold the private practice and has moved on to other challenges and is now focused on his/her stamp in life.

Or possibly the Hall of Fame Owner has passed up the opportunity to sell and is still in the game because of a deep passion for private practice physical therapy.

The Hall of Fame Owner is involved in advocacy, possibly teaching future PTs or other private practice owners and is establishing a legacy through helping other people.

The Hall of Fame Owner's staff may even be a touch smarter than the Hall of Famer because of a willingness to attract and surround himself with great people...super smart, intelligent and loyal problem solvers who are solution-focused. He/she humbly knows that there are better experts out there.

The Hall of Fame Owner may now be more concerned and focused on his/her own purpose for himself, his life, his practice, his business, his family, his health, etc.

The Hall of Fame Owner has now likely helped many others along the way. Most likely without any fanfare or seeking any recognition.

The Hall of Fame Owner is recognized, admired and sought after as a mentor and reaps from places he/she did not even remember sowing.

The Hall of Fame Owner has well established and tested marketing pathways in place to attract ideal clients and has a consistent effort to expand on products and services to offer to clients. The practice likely includes other services and successful businesses than physical therapy outside of the typical PT industry.

The Hall of Fame Owner realizes that he and his team were his own best investment.

HALL OF FAMER

1. Has **multiple marketing magnets** on cruise control attracting exponentially more clients and providing even more services to them.
2. M.O. - "Unconscious Competence."
3. They will say things like, "**Who can we find and get wisdom from? And who can we give it to?**"
4. **Focused on the riches of life** not just financial and business success.
5. **Advocate for the Profession**

A Recap of the 4 Levels...

First, we covered the Minor Leaguer. It is usually marked by one or no established tested marketing pathways. They are focused on their own certifications, clinical education and being an owner.

There is the Major Leaguer who believes there are a limited number of referral sources in any geographical area and they end up chasing referrals.

The All-Star has multiple established marketing systems in place and those systems are tested.

The Hall of Famer has multiple marketing magnets on cruise control attracting exponentially more clients and providing even more services to them.

A review of the M.O., dilemma and finance for each level...

The Minor Leaguer is **unconscious incompetence.** They say things like, *"If I could just make a little more money."* In the beginning they are overly confident then they become overwhelmed. They usually have no reserves and they are compiling debt.

The Major Leaguer is **conscious incompetence.** They will say things like, *"If I just had more time."* They have fear of future losses then they become angry and jaded. They are usually a high income earner with little or no equity.

The All-Star is **conscious competence.** They usually say, *"Now what?"* They have a healthy curiosity then possibly boredom. They have usually no debt and adequate cash reserves. They can afford affluence. They are not worried about money and they have systems for finances.

The Hall of Famer is **unconscious competence.** They will say things like, *"Who can we find and get wisdom from? And who can we give it to?"*

The Hall of Famer is now focused on the riches of life not just financial and business success.

So where are you at?

If you took an honest assessment of yourself and your private practice, where are you?

Likely, as you were reading through this chapter, there were things that resonated with you and where you are at in your life.

Which one best describes you?

At the bottom of the page here, just write down the level of private practice that you are at right now.

And more importantly, where do you want to be?

Do you want to move up and literally take the next step to the next level and become a Major Leaguer or an All-Star? Or do you have aspirations to one day have a Hall of Famer career? Is that your true aspiration?

Again, write that down below.

More importantly, what is your plan for getting there?

You likely picked up this book to learn more about marketing. So let's get started with the basics of private practice marketing.

Where Are You Now?.. **Date:** ....

Where Do You Want to Be?.................................... **By When?** ....

Chapter 6

Marketing 101...
What They Don't Teach Us in PT School

The Four Scientific Marketing Fundamentals You Need to Know if You Want to Be Successful in Private Practice

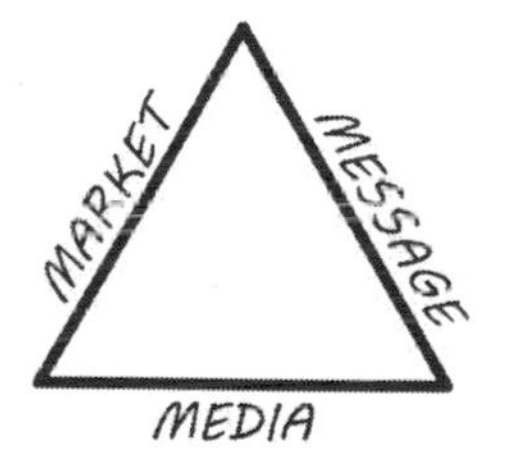

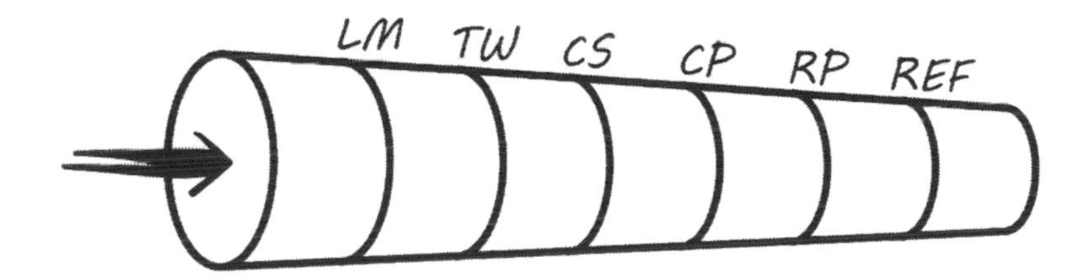

The first marketing fundamental that you need to know is direct response marketing.

Just like we are taught to be scientific in the clinic with our treatments...you can be scientific with your marketing...

For example, evidence-based practice is a big deal right now – we read research-based journals. We read research articles. We take continuing education classes and earn CEUs. All in the intention of providing more efficient, more effective treatment that produces better outcomes for our patients and our referral sources.

You can do that same exact thing in marketing.

If you are a scientist in the clinic, why not be a scientist with your marketing?

The answer to that, the way to be scientific, is direct response marketing.

For a reference for this, you can go the whole way back to the early 1900's and read Claude Hopkins' *Scientific Marketing*, which specifically covers the key components of direct response marketing.

For a free pdf of *Scientific Marketing*...
email me at **chad@breakthroughptmarketing.com**...
and type "Scientific Marketing" in the email subject line.

This concept has been around for over 150 years. It has been used very effectively.

There are a couple of components that you should know about with regards to direct response marketing...

The first is there is going to be an offer. There will always be an offer within your marketing pieces from here on out.

What Most of Us Do When Busy...Roulette Marketing

That is significantly different from branding, where typically what most of us do as private practice owners is we do the roulette marketing...

We are extremely busy. We don't call marketing companies to come into our clinic, but they usually stop by. They are with the radio station, the TV station, the local newspaper and they are selling marketing.

And we buy it (sometimes because we are just so busy and want them to leave us alone).

So we commit to the marketing.

The deadline then approaches and now it is time for us to crank something out.

The thing that most of us commonly resort to is throwing our logo and slogan in the ad.

Call us at 555-1234, we will include our clinic phone number.

We will list our clinic website and then we will say silly things like "visit us on Facebook and Twitter and YouTube" and all of this other stuff.

And it doesn't work...

Then when we go back to it later, when we come back around, we wonder why that didn't work.

We are going to talk more about that in a second...

In this case, for direct response marketing, realize that you are always going to have a very specific offer in every ad that you ever run from here on out.

The second component is there is always a call to action, hence the phrase "direct response".

So really what we want is when we advertise our services - whether it be online, whether it be in print, whether it be in a postcard or direct mail... however we chose to advertise...whatever media we select - we always want a call to action.

We always want people with that specific problem to raise their hand and say, *"Yes, I want help for this."*

The other nice thing is the third part of direct response marketing, that is always going to be prevalent, is that you get to choose your target market.

For us, in our private practice, we have wanted to change our payer mix for the longest time. (Who doesn't, right?!)

Once I began applying direct response marketing in my private practice, I realized very quickly that I could go and target a more affluent population. That I just didn't have to market to every single person who lived close to my clinic. I could get very scientific about it and I could, for example, market specifically to households that had at least 2 people living in it and had $100,000 or more in household income.

Very, very basic...but you get to choose that.

Would you rather attract somebody into your physical therapy practice who cannot afford their copay? Or would you rather attract somebody who can?

I think that the answer is pretty obvious there. You want the latter. Somebody who is not going to be very resistant to their copay issue and they are going to be willing to invest in their own body and their health and wellness.

The fourth component of direct response marketing is anonymity. Your ad can be anonymous. The stress isn't on your logo. The emphasis isn't on branding or top of mind awareness...(which I have never seen a branding ad beat a direct response marketing ad ever, ever, ever in my private practice.)

The nice thing is the emphasis is on serving the person who is raising their hand and not on how "pretty" my logo is.

I think you will discover the same if you truly do A/B split testing with direct response marketing versus any branding ad that you have ever done in the past.

The Magic Formula: Market-Message-Media Match

A year or so ago, I did a survey of literally thousands of private practice owners all over the US.

We asked the question, "What mistakes have you made in private practice marketing?"

Inevitably, 100% of all answers focused on media.

The private practice owners listed print ads, social media including Facebook, Twitter, YouTube, Google ads, SEO, newspaper ads, magazine ads, sponsorship ads in soccer team programs, radio, and television to name a few...

Absolutely anything that you can imagine.

Here is the deal though... the only thing that they focused on - that we all focus on in terms of marketing - is the media that we are buying.

That is unfortunate because there is another big secret... the big key often isn't in the media.

We blame it on the media.

(That is the importance of this concept as you will quickly discover here in Market-Message-Media Match.)

Dan Kennedy is a direct response marketing expert with over 40 years of experience. You have probably heard of him if you read any business books. He is famous for the *No B.S.* series of books on marketing and *The Ultimate Marketing Plan.*

He also has a course that I have done and I highly recommend to other business owners, let alone private practice owners. It is called **Magnetic Marketing.** That is his flagship course. It is excellent. It covers direct response marketing.

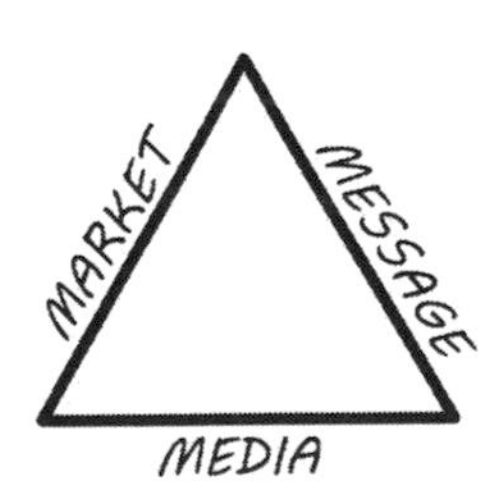

Dan came up with the principle of Market-Message-Media Match. (And if he wasn't the originator...he certainly has done the most to promote the concept).

I just want to go through and define each one and how it works as well, per Dan Kennedy.

If we define **Market**...market is the people that we are targeting.

In a second, we are going to get to the 3 target markets in private practice PT, but just realize if you are in an area, let's say there are 100,000 people within 25 miles of your office...

You can certainly go to the unwashed masses and market to every single person that lives in your area, which would be a geographic target market.

Or you can select married women between the ages of 45 and 65 who have 2 or more children and live in households with $100,000 or more a year in household income.

That would be one possible target market.

So you can see how you can get very, very specific with who you are looking to target.

So that is market.

The next one is **Message.**

There are a couple of formulas that I have learned in the reference books that I just gave you (which would be the Dan Kennedy and Claude Hopkins books)...

There is a way to craft a marketing message that most of us in private practice PT have never learned and we struggle to write in ways that our target market is going to understand.

So many times, what we will do is, what we learned in physical therapy school was you study a topic...

For example, I remember my graduate year I had to do a presentation on MS, multiple sclerosis. So I went and studied that topic. Then I did a 50 minute presentation. (I think we did it in group format and presented to the rest of my classmates.) I'm pretty sure that I got an A on the project, which was great. But if I turn around and try to use that same exact information (which is what most of us do and which I did early on as well in marketing) to people that are diagnosed with MS, that same presentation wouldn't be nearly as effective.

Because talking from PT to PT is a lot different than talking PT to a potential patient.

Again, most of us fail in crafting a message in the language of the people we're trying to reach...

If I had to go back to every single practice owner who responded to "The mistakes in our practice marketing" survey, where they blamed it on the media...almost every single time the mistake truly is in the message...

Even with private practice owners that I work with, many times they will take something that I do exactly and they will tell me, "Chad, I did it exactly as you do it...and it didn't work..."

Then I look at what they have done and they have changed the message. They somehow put in a big fancy physical therapy term such as spondylolisthesis and they didn't keep it simple in layperson's terminology and keep the message very effective and pure.

The third component is **Media.**

Again this can be pretty much infinite, but there are a lot of different types of media.

Right now all the rage is email marketing and social media because they are sexy.

They are relatively inexpensive to advertise through, if not completely free.

However, there is a lot of media to choose from...

We are still getting very effective outcomes from direct mail, in particular using direct response.

So direct mail can work.

Postcards can work.

Radio can work.

Television can work.

Just about everything that you can imagine in regards to media can work... if you match the right media to the right market with the right message...

The idea is to test it and find the right media that matches your target market. If my target market is... let's say that we are going to get very narrow and say 45 to 55 year-old married females, you want to say to yourself, what type of media do they utilize...do they buy from?

I just read a recent marketing story in a really good book called *Ask* by Ryan Levesque.

In it, he talks about a healthcare company who believed their target market was 45 to 55-year-old men. When they went back and surveyed who was actually buying...most of the buyers were actually 55 to 65-year-old men.

So what they did is they went back and crafted a message for a different decade. One that emphasized when 55 to 65 year olds were growing up.

This healthcare company crafted a message around what it was like to be growing up, if you were 65 years old, nostalgia would be like when you were 16... so they talked about Ford Mustangs and muscle cars relative to that era. They matched the market...

So that is really, really important. You always want to make sure that you are matching the type of media that is being used and the message with the market.

So if you match all three, if you get all three right and they resonate with each other and they are correct, you are going to have success. If you get one wrong, you are going to experience failure...or at least a lesser return on your investment (R.O.I.) than you could've experienced otherwise...

For example, I have found it very hard to market in any way whatsoever, that is in any way effective on Twitter.

I have 3,000+ followers, but my target market - which is 45 to 55-year-old married women - do not use Twitter.

They are not tweeting.

They are not putting stuff out in 140 characters and catching up with what their friend's children and grandchildren are doing.

They are not using that to communicate.

It is the wrong media for my market.

If you get one of those wrong, your target market, your message or the media, you are going to experience failure.

That is the importance of Market-Message-Media Match per Dan Kennedy.

Since we talked about target markets, I want to give you the 3 big target markets...

This is the third marketing fundamental that you need to know.

The 3 Big Target Markets for Private Practice PT

Physicians

Number one, which is what I relied on early on, there is a huge misnomer that I think still exists in private practice misunderstanding... we do not need physician referrals to stay in business.

However, they are nice.

There is still a segment of the population who believes "whatever" their doctor tells them.

Marketing to Physicians is not something that we have completely abandoned.

It no longer makes up the majority of the business coming into my private practice, but it is something that I still respect and I think it is there...

The first target market is **Physicians...**

In this, I am going to lump together Nurse Practitioners, PAs (Physician's Assistants) and any other healthcare provider that can legally refer to physical therapy in your state.

So that may also be dentistry, Podiatrists, (I know Physical Therapists who get referrals from Chiropractors)...we have had personal trainers refer to us...we have had Massage Therapists refer to us...even though we will end up seeing that patient via Direct Access.

But it is basically anybody who works in healthcare who is a potential referral.

(We have also received referrals from Neurologists, Ophthalmologists, Ear, Nose and Throat Doctors... just about any specialty that you can imagine, including the classic Orthopedic or Spine Surgeon.)

Patients

The second target market that I want to cover is your **Patients.**

This includes your past and present patient base.

*****The lowest hanging fruit in private practice marketing is people who already know, like and trust you.**

Hopefully if you are providing high quality of care, then your patients are more than willing to respond to any other offer that you have.

If you have followed the news at all, you have seen companies selling for millions of dollars...often times for 100's of millions of dollars...

In nearly every single one of those cases, what the larger company is buying is usually the customer list.

Well, the thing that I see that 99% of private practice owners ignore is their present and past patients.

They are constantly trying to leave the faucet on with physician referrals. But sometimes they will even unconsciously block those patients once they are in from coming back in the future.

I know myself that I am guilty of this. Early on in my private practice career, my physical therapy career, I would say things like, *"Hey, you met all of your goals. You are doing great. Hopefully I don't see you again."* Or something along those lines...

That is very foolish, because people who we have helped with shoulder impingement... when they have back pain 3 years from now... are much more likely, and we hope it to be true, that they are much more likely to return to us for their care rather than look through Google for physical therapy in our area.

We want them to come back to us.

So the second target market that you can market to is your **present and past patient base.**

And recognize the value of that list. It is likely one of the most valuable things that you have in your private practice from a business perspective.

Public

The third target market is the **Public.**

This has received increased attention over the last 10 years, specifically with the APTA's Vision 2020.

I want to share a quick comment on Direct Access here because I believe that is what most of us are trying to do in private practice is attract more Direct Access patients from the general public rather than relying on physician referrals...

Direct Access is a destination for Physical Therapists. It is not a destination for patients.

They don't care if we have Direct Access or not. It is not a benefit.

The benefit they seek is that they get to enjoy the activities that they want to do.

If they want to sit on the floor and play with their grandchildren...or they get to keep running...or they get to return to work without back pain. They get to reach up into the cupboard or get to do household work or yard work or stand or walk or sit without pain.

That is the benefit.

That is the destination for the patient in the patient's mind.

The destination is not Direct Access.

However, done scientifically, you can attract Direct Access patients from the general public without ever saying "Direct Access." We have learned to do it quite well.

In a later chapter on Workshops, I will be sharing with you one specific tool that you can input into your private practice and hopefully realize the same success that I have had and that the other private practice physical therapy owners that I have shared this with have had.

But for now, realize that those are the 3 target markets:

1. **Physicians and potential referral sources in the medical community**
2. **Your past and present Patients**
3. **The general Public**

The Patient Experience Funnel

There are 6 steps here and I am going to go through each one of them very briefly and give you a description of what they are.

Then I am also going to give you the 3 biggest mistakes with regards to the Patient Experience Funnel.

Here are the 6 steps...

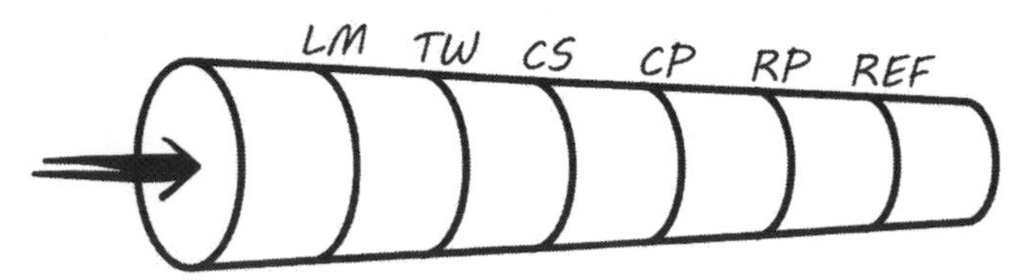

1. Lead Magnet

A lead magnet is a free piece of valuable information. It can be consumed in a short period of time that essentially gets somebody to raise their hand and say, *"Yes, I have _____* (fill in the blank with back pain, shoulder pain, vestibular issues, problems walking, pain with sitting and standing, whatever it may be)."

But somebody from your target market raises their hand and says, "*Yes, I have that.*"

Most commonly, these are pieces of information.

There are 3 things that you can offer as a lead magnet... 3 categories:

1. **A product**
2. **A service**
3. **Information**

What I see a lot of private practice owners doing... the majority of them doing that are exploring direct response marketing at all... is they are offering a Free Exam upfront. (I've heard this called a Discovery Appointment or Discovery Session or Test Drive...none-the-less you get the idea...it's all the same).

I think that is a huge mistake.

I think you are much better off, and I know that you are much better off, if you offer some sort of information first.

So what is information as a lead magnet?

It could be a video.

It could be a book.

It could be a report.

Something simple that they can download and realize, *"This Physical Therapist knows what I have and they know my story and ultimately I want to seek out care from them".*

So we will talk more about how to do that...

But let's move on...

2. Tripwire

So once somebody has raised their hand, we want to discern if they are a "tire kicker"...

(That means that they are just looking around and they are NEVER going to commit to physical therapy and become a patient.)

Or whether it is your ideal client...

Somebody who is willing to overcome the barriers of time, money and distance to receive your care. And is going to walk in and respect what you have to say about their condition and be compliant with their program, their plan of care and achieve their goals and then go out and tell other people.

The way we do that is with a device called a tripwire.

What that is it is another piece of (usually) information, although it can be a service or a product that involves a small commitment of time or money.

For example, many times I will see a book used where it is free plus shipping and handling...(most likely how you got your hands on this book!)

It is the most common one used now, but there are others.

We have done a workshop, which is a free lead magnet-type product, then after the workshop, we drive to the free exam.

If somebody shows up for the free exam, they are willing to take time to invest in their own health and wellness. They made a time commitment so we realize that there is a really good chance that they are not just kicking the tires.

Think about what they have done...they read an ad.

They responded.

They called the office.

They registered for the workshop.

They showed up to the workshop.

We have them fill out a worksheet... They filled out the worksheet.

And now they have said, *"Yes, I want more help. I believe that you can help me. Let me schedule an appointment."*

That is a fairly effective tripwire as well.

So a tripwire is something that has a small time or money commitment.

You are delineating and discerning between the tire kickers and someone who is serious about becoming a patient.

3. Core Service
So this is the 97001.

It is the 97110, 97140 and the other CPT codes that you are billing for your physical therapy service.

I don't think I need to cover that any more extensively than just realizing that it is the physical therapy service that you are providing... whether you are in a cash pay or insurance-based private practice.

4. Cash Pay, Upsells or Profit Maximizers
Realize that once somebody has gone through their physical therapy service, there are other services that we can offer that person now that they know, like and trust us.

The most common are small group training or personal training, personal fitness classes, health and wellness information and massage.

Most private practice owners that I talk with who are doing anything at all on the backend of their Patient Experience Funnel... they are either doing something related to fitness, nutrition or a massage-type service.

5. Return Path
This is where customers who have already bought from you in the past are returning to you now for additional care.

So Mary, for example, had a total knee replacement a year ago. She graduated physical therapy. She went home and she was pleased. And now she is having hip pain. She is coming back in to see you for hip pain.

That is the return path.

Past patients who are returning to your physical therapy practice for additional care.

6. Referrals

The best place to get referrals is from your past patient base.

Customers who are happy are much more likely to share with other potential customers. The neat thing is that socioeconomically, they tend to hang out with people who are just like them...

So the best place to attract like-minded patients and like-minded customers is your past patient base.

That is referrals.

Here in a minute, we will talk about return path and referrals and how you can do that with a patient newsletter...

The 3 Most Common Mistakes I See in Private Practice

The first mistake is no soft landing.

So there is no lead magnet, no tripwire at all.

Again we will go back to the example of if you walked in a room for a 97001 and you asked the patient, *"Why are you here?"* And the patient said, *"Because my doctor sent me."* That is no soft landing.

So that person hasn't consumed any lead magnet that you have had out there. They haven't consumed any tripwires. They are basically there because their physician sent them.

Most practice owners don't offer any lead magnets or any tripwires at all.

Any brochures or information that they have out basically yell, *"I'm great. Here is why we are awesome. Here is what we specialize in. This is all of the schooling that we have had."* ...rather than focusing on the direct response marketing concept of providing value to the potential client first.

When that is done correctly, there is an indoctrination that happens where the person walks in and they hold you with a lot more respect than if that soft landing is not there.

So you want people to consume your lead magnets and your tripwires before they walk in for their 97001.

The second mistake is thinking about your business or your private practice in terms of **core service only.**

It is kind of like tunnel vision... most private practice owners are trying to make 100% of their profitability within that core service.

However, if we look at mistake #3, which is **no long-term customer value concept**, we can quickly see that the private practices of the future are going to understand this.

They are going to be willing to break even on the core service in order to make profitability with the cash pay, return path and referrals.

Also, they are going to look at and consider the long-term customer value of every client that they see.

So if you do have and decide to build out the back of your Patient Experience Funnel, there is much less stress on trying to create massive profitability in the core service alone.

In smart practices...what happens is your tripwire or your lead magnet may break even, or even lose a little bit of money, in order for you to gain a customer who ultimately buys the plan of care and consumes the other backend services that you have in addition to physical therapy. The backend of the Patient Experience Funnel is where the majority of the profitability is made...

So the successful private practices of the future are going to realize and utilize the full **6 Step Patient Experience Funnel.**

Chapter 7

Phase I – Fixing Your Funnel

Minimizing Leaks Before You Buy Marketing Traffic

Before you rush out and start buying various marketing pathways and media...for example, Facebook, Google ads, print ads, postcards, etc....you'll want to make sure that your funnel is super tight so that you maximize the return on your investment.

From a study of over 200 owners that have gone through my Killer Marketing Training, we noticed a very strong trend which is as follows:

The Owners who got the best results when they began going out to buy media and marketing their practices...**first fixed their funnel.**

We narrowed it down to these 4 steps:

1. **The Green Ink Letter**
2. **The 7 Step Killer Exam**
3. **The Killer Testimonial Machine**
4. **The Greatest Promotion Ever**

Right now, I will go through each one of these and how you can apply them to your practice.

Obviously we don't have infinite room here within a book, but I will give you the biggest points, at least, for each tool.

1. The Green Ink Letter

What the Green Ink Letter is in a nutshell is a personal letter from you, the Physical Therapist, to somebody who is either a patient or somebody who has referred a patient to you. (Either a referral source or a past patient.)

Why is it green?

I will give you that story right now...

In my business career, I have had three business mentors.

Two of them recommended this same exact tool to me.

It's what ultimately became the Green Ink letter.

(In the beginning, I called it "the Gary Lee Houck, Sr. letter.")

It is a small personal note, again from you the PT, to the patient or to the referral source that follows these three steps:

Step 1 is to acknowledge or recognize.

For example, let's say we treated Mary for 12 visits for her total knee replacement and she is now graduated. On the day of discharge, I would write a Green Ink letter to Mary and I would say something like this:

"Mary, it was a pleasure to work with you in physical therapy for your knee. I'm amazed at how far you have come from the first day that you walked in here. I really hope you have a great day at the beach with your grandchildren in February. Sincerely, Chad. P.S. By the way, if you need to contact me for anything, the best way to reach me is (I would give either my phone number, my direct office line or perhaps my cell number or my email address at work.)"

Let's take a look at what we just did there.

One, we acknowledged and recognized Mary for following through with her plan of care, achieving her goals of getting back to normal again and getting her life back.

Two, we had a personal comment in there that we were paying attention to what was important to her...we recognized that she was going to the beach with her grandchildren and when that was.

Three, we have a very soft call to action at the end.

You want to hit those 3 steps whether you are writing to a referral source or a patient.

Let's give you an example for a referral source as well.

Let's say the day that we see somebody for the first time and we bill a 97001 on an IE...

I would typically say something like this to the referral source:

"Hi Doctor Smith, I wanted to thank you for the referral of Mary. I saw her for the first time in the clinic today. She did really well on her first visit. I will keep you updated on her progress. Sincerely, Chad. P.S. Please send more like her."

The one question that I will commonly get asked is why green?

Well it just so happens that in my private practice logo the dominant colors are green, yellow and orange. Green is the only one of those colors that shows up well in writing on stationery.

So that is why we went with green.

It doesn't necessarily have to be green, but I can tell you that you want something that stands out.

I know in national tests, blue on yellow or canary yellow background wins many split tests...if you really want to be scientific about how you are doing this.

2. The 7 Step Killer Exam

What the 7 Step Killer Exam does is it walks you through step-by-step from the introduction when you walk in and meet a patient for the first time during their initial evaluation (or during their free screen or discovery appointment, discovery session whatever you want to call it), the whole way through them signing up for and scheduling their full plan of care when they are in agreement with what successful treatment looks like.

Again, I don't really have the space in the book here to cover every single step, but I want to at least share the two most important steps with you.

One is an important question that needs to be asked during the history portion of the exam before you ever provide any treatment at all...

It is asking this question, *"Have you ever had physical therapy before?"*

This is the importance of asking the question: If they have had a good experience with physical therapy in the past...fantastic.

By the way, when you and I say "physical therapy," it could mean any one of the following things - which I have heard from patients... it could be that they saw an athletic trainer or that they saw a Chiropractor or that they were treated with manual therapy from their DO. They may be thinking massage therapy. I have had patients refer to P90X as "doing their physical therapy."

It could be any one of those things that they are equating physical therapy to.

They are walking in with preconceived notions of what physical therapy is.

You want to find out whether those preconceived notions are good or bad related to PT.

If it is positive and they did really well with it in the past...then that's a bonus...

If they had a negative experience, you want to uncover that right away.

Here is the best part about it, you don't even have to do anything with it.

You don't have to sell yourself.

You don't have to position yourself against Chiropractors or against physical therapy down the street.

The only thing that you have to do is acknowledge and recognize that they have had an experience and it was a negative experience. If it was negative, you just have to hear it out.

You do that simply by saying, "Ok, can you tell me what happened?"

They will relay their story and then you get to the end of that and you say, "Ok, thank you for sharing that."

So for example, let's say somebody went down the street and they paid $3,000 for 20 visits of decompression at the Chiropractor and they didn't do really well.

They just felt that somebody left them in the room for 45 minutes, never checked on them and they had a really negative experience. And it made their pain worse, at least in their own perspective.

The only thing that you want to do, you don't want to bash Chiropractic care.

You don't want to bash anybody individually.

You just want to say, "*Mary, I want to thank you for sharing that story with me. I will make sure that does not happen when you are here.*"

That is the end of it.

But it is a really important step for you to go through and pick that up and just listen to that. Most people as patients have never had that experience before, you want to provide it for them.

The second important step during the exam that I want to share with you is—especially in the days now of cash pay PT, extremely high copays and very large deductibles in the thousands of dollars—we want to make sure that we are showing that we can provide an effective outcome.

This isn't going to happen 100% of the time, but you at least want to show an effort in doing so.

Test, Treat, Retest

What I mean by that is let's say that we are seeing somebody for back pain. We go through and see that they are limited to 5° of extension. They feel 8/10 pain. I'm going to do my treatment... whether it is manual therapy, whether it is providing another modality or taking them through directional preference exercises... then I'm going to retest.

I want to get them to the point of saying, *"Wow, that is better."*

I aim to do that on the first session and every single session with every single patient I treat in PT.

And I think you should be doing the same.

At the end, if you do this the right way and you do the 7 steps and you touch all of the bases, what will happen when you get to the plan of care summary, you are going to sign it and the patient is going to sign it.

You now have something in writing that you have both said, *"Here is what we are working towards (in the patient's language). This is the cause of the problem and this is what successful treatment looks like."*

You both sign it and it serves as a consent to treatment and the patient walks away with a copy of that.

What that does is it prevents and minimizes patients falling off during their plan of care.

You are now both on the same page working towards the same goals...and you have it in writing.

(The primary benefit is psychological...not legal).

3. The Killer Testimonial Machine

Have you ever noticed that at the end when somebody graduates or when you discharge them to a home exercise program...they will gladly bring you in baked goods...perhaps a tray of their famous homemade cookies or their brownies or a pie or some other sort of gift?

Have you ever wondered how you can convert that energy into something positive for your overall clinic rather than just adding calories in the break room for your staff?

Well the answer to that is the **Killer Testimonial Machine.**

It is a way to gather a written story as part of the medical record that you can then turn around, with approval of the patient, and use for marketing and attracting other patients just like them.

When Mary graduates PT and she brings in her famous blueberry rhubarb pie, there is a certain energy there.

She knows, likes and trusts you. She has a story. She likely did really well with PT or otherwise she wouldn't be bringing in a pie to thank you.

You just want to convert that energy and have her share her positive experience.

(Obviously- don't turn down the pie.)

Here is how we do that:

On the day of the patient's graduation, we take objective measurements... then at the end of the final visit...to get a subjective story, we have a clipboard in every therapist's area with a pen and a sheet ready to go that simply asks for the patient to state in their own words how they did in physical therapy - focusing on what they couldn't do before PT and what they can do now.

They fill that out.

The sheet is designed to be open-ended. (Not a traditional, multiple choice survey)...

Two Types of Testimonials

You are going to have patients that write a 5 word sentence and that is all that they will write... and that's fine.

And you are going to have patients that write paragraph after paragraph about their experience in physical therapy.

You take both. I never ask a patient to rewrite or anything like that.

How This Can Help You

Then what we do with that is we send a copy of that back to the referring physician with the discharge report. And what we have now built over the years is literally thousands upon thousands of testimonials that we can use depending on what we want to attract.

So if we want to advertise for back pain, we literally have 3,000 or more back pain testimonials that we can pull from.

And going back to that Market-Message-Media Match from the previous chapter, if we want to match the market and we are advertising to 65+-year-old seniors, we can pull a testimonial from a back pain patient who is age 65 or older.

If we are doing something for golfers, we can pull one for golfing from a golfer we treated.

The beauty of the system is you just want an exponentially growing number of referrals.

And what it does also is when you send it to the referral source, many times they will just simply read that...and ignore or skim the full Discharge Report.

What it does is it justifies the referral in the mind of the referral source. It makes them feel good about the referral and encourages them to do more.

As we know, technology is changing very rapidly. Presently, as I am writing this book, there are tools to take the testimonial and encourage social media sharing...

And for that reason, I'm hesitant to share them here...

Probably the easiest way to find out what is new in Private Practice Social Media Marketing is to go to **www.breakthroughptmarketing.com** and check out what we're doing there.

Before we cover the 4th System in Phase I...2 Real Life Results from Other Owners in the Trenches...

Is 400% Year to Year Growth Even Possible?

"In October 2014, I was leaving another physician meeting feeling frustrated with our company growth and I realized that I did not have control of my business. I was 8 months into growing my physical therapy clinic, Acadiana Pain & Performance Rehab, in Lafayette, LA. Lafayette, with a population of 120-150,000, has more than 30 physical therapy clinics. The dense competition, along with the growing issue of physician-owned practices,

was making consistent growth difficult. I was having a hard time getting doctors to increase referrals despite doing lunches, drop-ins, etc. For the month of October 2014, I saw 140 patient visits. At that same time, I decided that I needed to make a change in the way we were marketing. I came across an article about how to market directly to patients and not be so reliant on physician marketing.

The first thing that I implemented from the Killer Marketing system was the Green Ink Letter. I sat down and wrote a small note to all of our recently discharged patient. This served 2 purposes... contact the patients we had in the past year and give them a soft call to action to tell their friends and family about us. With only this step, we saw an increase in patients of about 40 extra visits in November, a shortened month. I soon began to implement the system step-by-step starting with the Green Ink Letter, then the 7 Step Evaluation, the Killer Testimonial Machine, Patient Newsletter, Physician Newsletter, patient intake packages, Health Mentor Club with certificates, Health Mentor Luncheon... and at that point we had to stop our progression into our full marketing program because we could not keep up and were running out of space at my current clinic.

The progression from day one just made perfect sense to me. I started my clinic to give people more comprehensive and personal pain rehab. The Killer Marketing system gave me a way to market in a more personal and patient-centered way. We were able to shift our focus to the patients we were serving and much less to the physician as traditionally done. In the ONE year after starting to implement and use the Killer Marketing strategies, we consistently saw 20-50% growth from month to month and in October of 2015 we saw 566 patient visits - a 400% year/year growth.

The implementation was not a cake walk. I had to change the way I was running things. Early on I began studying from 6:00am–7:00am on Monday mornings to go through that week's module. I would make notes and then meet with staff on Wednesdays for an hour to go through new implementation needed. There was a good bit of extra work on me and the staff, but it was paying off so quickly everyone was excited. I told Chad on a call that my favorite thing about the Killer Marketing system was that my stress and worry of whether we were going to make it was gone. I now felt that I had control of my patient load, business and growth. That was worth everything to me. We are not done and we will definitely continue to get better, but we know where we are going and how we are going to get there."

– **Derrick Hines,** Louisiana

"Prior to joining BPTM, I knew nothing about marketing, and had no system for marketing in my 25-year-old private practice. With physician referrals decreasing yearly, it was obvious I needed to do something in order for the clinic to grow. I knew that I didn't like the idea of "selling" or "begging for referrals." Throwing money aimlessly at random advertising was something I was unwilling to do.

When I started with BPTM, I discovered the basics of marketing: terms, approaches, processes. It was like Marketing Anatomy and Physiology. The material was focused on direct-response marketing using scientific principles and measuring results. I was drawn to the idea of implementing specific, strategic, tested-and-proven marketing tools.

During the year that I have been with BPTM, I would now consider myself a marketing believer and convert. I am fascinated by the research, technology, and opportunities for private practice physical therapy.

The first tool I implemented was the Killer Testimonial Machine. It is EASY, ECONOMICAL, and EVERGREEN (many uses, never gets old).

We now have over 100 killer testimonials on our walls, and another 50 on deck, waiting for room.

Prospective patients are drawn to these walls, which reinforces the social proof of our services.

New and returning patients are led down the Hall of Fame, which is covered with patient stories, on their way to the exam rooms and gym. Many are excited to find people they know on the walls. Those that are in need of encouragement, receive it by reading the stories of those that have been there.

Staff motivation has improved since implementing the Killer Testimonial Machine. The stories, which tell the before and after of receiving physical therapy, often acknowledge many of the staff members, and serve as a letter of gratitude by the patient.

We use the testimonials as part of our marketing system in online and offline campaigns - website, Facebook, direct mail offers, and newsletters.

Last year, we achieved a 37% increase in revenues from the prior year. While we did work to improve our other systems as well, the majority of that increase is directly related to implementing the marketing systems from BPTM."

– **Stacey Raybuck Schatz,** Massachusetts

4. The Greatest Promotion Ever

The last thing that I want to talk with you, the 4th System in Phase I, is something that I call "The Greatest Promotion Ever"...

Why I Created the Greatest Promotion Ever

What was happening for us was year after year in my private practice in the 4th quarter...we would experience a dip.

My first big and painful 4th quarter loss was in 2007...I had about a $44,000 loss of income minus expense.

Our monthly new patients in that one quarter, went from about 154 in October to 106 in November to 66 in December.

We crashed pretty hard.

You would have thought that I learned my lesson from that low point, but I did not.

Two years later, I made a similar business mistake...we ended up with nearly a $100,000 loss of income minus expense.

After that...I wanted to do everything in my power to prevent that from happening ever again...

So I designed an event internally for us at Madden PT that would drive more patients in than we could treat...

And I have now started sharing that with other private practice owners who have had a lot of success with it as well.

Results of the Greatest Promotion Ever
Here is what happened...

The first year...rather than having the typical open house event we did in the past, we promoted a "celebration."

The celebration was different...and here's the key to this...we had a reason why to celebrate.

(You always want to have a reason why you are celebrating and why you are having an event.)

Then we opened it up for a day of free screenings.

For us, we always hold it on a Tuesday morning for a 5 hour session...7 a.m. to 12 noon.

Year 1 we had 7 Physical Therapists available. So we ended up with 70 treatment slots. We saw 68 patients and we ended up scheduling 40 full plans of care from that.

Year 2 we only had 50 slots available (because we had one therapist out on maternity leave and another one retired). We ended up filling those 50 slots AND ended up with a waiting list.

Here is a quick success story from one of our owners... Anthony Sylvester.

He has been in practice in rural Oklahoma for about 22 years...

For his Greatest Promotion Ever, he mailed out 300 pieces for $260

Anthony's practice had 21 converted patients, plus a waiting list of 11!

Pretty cool stuff.

The Important Parts for Your Greatest Promotion Ever

The promotion that you are sending out...realize it's very difficult during your typical slow season to increase referrals from physicians or increase referrals from general public.

Specifically for those of us in Private Practice, in the 4th quarter between Thanksgiving and Christmas...we are competing for eyeballs with companies that have a much bigger marketing spend than our private practice does... for example, Target and Best Buy...

So we avoid focusing too much on Physicians and the General Public target markets to save us...

We go straight to our past patient base because it's the low hanging fruit.

What we have done is we position our Greatest Promotion Ever immediately before our typical slow season.

On Year 1, I believe that we had it on November 3rd...

What that did is it created a 7 week backlog of new patients waiting to get in that took us to January 7th of the following year to catch up.

So the Greatest Promotion Ever has been extremely powerful for us.

We have now run it 5 times and it has been successful at creating a backlog of patients.

A Phase I Recap of the 4 Fix Your Funnel Systems

These are the 4 tools that you want to go through before you go out and you buy any more marketing for your private practice.

1. **The Green Ink Letter**
2. **The 7 Step Killer Exam**
3. **The Killer Testimonial Machine**
4. **The Greatest Promotion Ever**

These 4 tools make up Phase I of the Killer Marketing Training.

We call Phase I "Fix Your Funnel".

Relying Less on Physician Referrals and Being There for My Kids...

"My name is George Hess. I am the owner of Hess Physical Therapy - we have 2 locations here in the Pittsburgh, Pennsylvania area.

I was pretty stressed out at the end of 2014. My numbers were down half in one of my clinics...they had really dipped down.

Before the end of 2015, my numbers are already back up to where they were in 2012, which is where our highest point was in our company.

The Turnaround

I have not gone out to see one physician...I haven't been to a doctor's office since I have started with BPTM.

That is what is amazing... the direct response stuff and the direct response type of marketing, how much it has worked.

It is such a peace of mind to know that I can control the volume without having to rely on any group or physician. It just gives you a sense of stability.

One thing that was also important to me was I was just working so many hours when I started with Breakthrough...

I have kids that are involved in things and I wanted to be there with them...I wanted to see those things and not be so stressed out and not taking work home and working in the evening and stuff like that.

This has given me freedom. I have seen a huge increase in our numbers. I haven't had to rely on anyone other than the marketing that we are learning and doing with BPTM.

I have been able to NOT miss anything with my kids. I'm there for their functions...I'm there in the evenings...and I have the freedom to come and go as I want in the clinic.

It is a kind of indescribable feeling of security.

I was so insecure there for a little while. I'm like, 'Oh my God, things are spiraling down.' It went so good, so good, so good and then we were really down there.

But now I think we are going to take it to another level, in all honesty.

I would have to say that through all of the marketing stuff, if I look at it... yeah, some of my expenses have increased, but it doesn't compare to the profitability that it has brought in.

Those slight increases in expenses, the profit completely outweighs it. It was money that was definitely worth spending in order to get to where we are getting to.

One thing that I had not done prior was the patient newsletters.

That was something that was fairly new to our practice. We immediately had a really good response from that.

I know the first campaign that we did where we had a free promotional day that Chad had taught us how to do, I think that I had more than 30 people schedule for that day. And 20 of them became patients.

I have never had anything make that much of a dramatic increase from just doing one thing. It was a huge increase in revenue.

I know prior to that I was like, 'Oh I'm going to spend a couple of thousand dollars on this campaign, getting these newsletters and stuff out'....but when you see the return on your investment, I will spend 2 grand every month to make 20 or 30 grand extra for sure.

The patients that came in, they start to refer other people to you. So it is just a continuing of growth through doing those things.

These were all pretty much past patients that I had not seen in a while. So kind of getting reacquainted with them...it has worked really, really well.

That is another thing that I have learned from Chad in BPTM...

It is not just the marketing stuff which has been fantastic, but he talks a lot about systems and having systems in place.

I think that is something that I lacked at one time.

It is great if you can increase the volume... but if you don't have the proper systems in place, you are never going to get to where you want to get to.

I mean my ultimate goal (and I told Chad this) was to be more in a position where of overseeing and running things in the clinic, but not as much of the hands-on I was doing.

I was doing hands-on stuff, plus all of the administrative stuff, plus the marketing stuff...I was feeling overwhelmed at times. I had tried stepping back previously, and the numbers would crash.

I have really started implementing some of the systems that he has in place: how to train staff, what types of things that you want to do to get everybody on the same page and integrating staff meetings a little bit more and stuff like that...that is making a difference.

As far as spending money on learning, I have used certain other consulting companies in the past - some were good experiences and some weren't very good experiences.

When I first was going to sign on with Chad, I was a little bit skeptical, as I think any private practice owner is going to be...

But after you get your first couple of returns on some of the things that you learn in there, you know that this group knows what they are talking about...I want to get to a certain level and I really believe that with the results that I have gotten so far, that this will help me get to where I want to get to.

I'm a business person, so if I am losing money, I'm not going to continue to lose money. If I'm making the increases that I want to, it is money that is well spent. It is not just the revenue increases that I have seen, it is the freedom that it has also allowed me. You can't put a price tag on that in my opinion. That is absolutely invaluable.

I think I have pretty much implemented just about everything that they have taught me... Killer Testimonial Machine, Green Ink Letters, 7 Step Killer Exam, Greatest Promotion Ever, Patient Newsletters... and that is why we have had successful outcomes.

If you go through this program and you do what they are teaching you and not try to alter it too much, pretty much do exactly what they are doing... you will have successful outcomes too."

– **George Hess,** Pennsylvania

Want to join Derrick, Stacey, George and the rest of us
in taking your Private Practice to the next level?
Are you willing to put in the work to get there?

Join us at **www.breakthroughptmarketing.com/apply**

Chapter 8

Phase II - Killer Patient Newsletters

The Who, What, When, Where, Why and How of Communicating with Your Past Patient Base So You Get More Past Clients Returning and Patients Referring Other Patients

The question that I will commonly get when I am talking with an owner about the Greatest Promotion Ever is "How do I mail out the offer?"

What I am going to share with you here is how you can package the Greatest Promotion Ever and all of your promotions in a way that it is consumed by your past and present patient base and it is acted upon.

Why Stay in Contact with Your Present and Past Patients?

The first one that I want to cover here is "WHY?"

So "Why would you mail and keep in contact with your present and past patient list?"

Well the #1 asset in your Private Practice is most likely your Patient List.

There is value in your list. (And if there isn't...there absolutely needs to be for you to stay in business)...

When you see companies (often tech companies making the news)...being bought and sold for billions of dollars...every single time there is significant value in their list.

What the purchasing company is buying is the seller's list.

And it is infinitely more valuable if the list is warm.

We are going to talk here about how to do this... how to warm up your list and also how to get value in your list.

Why Use a Newsletter?

The biggest reasons that we want to communicate with our patient list via a newsletter is:

First, we want to increase the likelihood of past clients returning for additional care.

This could also be for offers other than just physical therapy such as massage, small group fitness, nutrition, anything like that...any additional service. We can have past clients that are cross-consuming those other services as well.

Second, we want our past patients and our customers to refer other people just like them.

Third, they will come to know, like and trust you...especially if you offer up a slice of who you are...what you stand for and what you believe in...

Your past patient list is the lowest hanging fruit in marketing your private practice. It is not only true in private practice; it is true in any business in just about any industry.

The people who have done business with you in the past, if they are satisfied and if they are happy, are much more likely to buy from you in the future.

The best way to make that happen is to share a little slice of your personal life... because people do business with people.

They want to know who you are...

They want to know the therapist who is treating them and a little slice of their personal life.

When we get into the Wizard of Oz template later, I will show you exactly how to do that.

Perhaps the biggest reason "why" is a story that just happened here in my private practice a few months ago...

We had a female in her mid 50's return for back pain. We hadn't seen her in over 9 years. (So 9 years ago she was seen for shoulder pain... now she returned for back pain.)

Her first comment in the waiting room when I saw her and recognized her was, *"It feels like I never left."*

That is exactly what you want to happen with your patient newsletter.

What Goes into Your Patient Newsletter?

Simply put, there are 3 components of your patient newsletter that you need to have for it to be the most successful.

The biggest mistake is that most private practice owners I see do a patient newsletter...they only include 1 of these components... and it is the section specifically about physical therapy.

Oddly enough it is probably the least important part...

So what are the 3 components?

1. **Irrelevant Content**
2. **Semi-relevant Content**
3. **Relevant Content (plus your offer)**

Irrelevant Content is a personal interest story.

Again, it is a share of a little slice of your personal life so that your patients feel as though they know you better and they are truly participating in a long-term relationship with you as their provider.

So some examples for what to share in this section...

I personally live on a farmette and we have personally shared stories about the 5 mini donkeys that we have. We have shared about chickens or gardening stories or trips with my family. Also, our Physical Therapists have shared personal stories as well.

BIG Nugget: The sharing of animals works really well because a large percentage of the population likes animals. So sharing animal stories is a good topic to cover in your irrelevant section.

Again, think about sharing a small section of your life that establishes a long-term relationship with the patient.

Another thing that we have done is dedicated entire newsletters to nothing more than irrelevant content. They have been some of our most successful pieces.

The second part is the **Semi-relevant Content.**

That is the connection between your personal interest story and your relevant content (which is 100% about physical therapy).

So things in this section may be recognizing or acknowledging a patient success story.

Maybe you can cover your group running a 5K race or participating in a fundraiser.

In our newsletter, we recognize patients who have referred other patients and we put their names in "bright lights" because we want to encourage exactly that...we want more patients to refer other patients.

We do a monthly "Health Mentor" luncheon where anybody who has referred a patient to us is invited to a monthly luncheon. We usually invite an outside speaker who comes in to talk on a specific topic.

So there are some of the examples of what you can cover in your semi-relevant content.

Another one is new staff. You can cover new staff in this section and introduce new staff to your past patient base.

The third aspect is the **Relevant Content**...or your offer.

This is what most of us know how to do as Physical Therapists.

The biggest mistake here is we often communicate it in a way that is in physical therapy language, not lay language.

For example, when I am running my Greatest Promotion Ever offer, we put it in this section.

The reason that we have labeled this the Wizard of Oz template is that the **irrelevant content** and the **semi-relevant content** are printed in black and white, and the **relevant content** and the offer is inserted in the middle and is in full color.

This is a small touch we do to make the offer stand out...

If you have ever seen the Wizard of Oz movie, the beginning of the movie is in black and white, the end of the movie is in black and white, and the middle of the movie is in color.

It's the same exact idea here.

We really want people to ultimately pay attention to the relevant offer.

If it pertains to them, we want them to consume that offer. We want them to call and schedule an appointment, call and schedule a free exam, call and register for a workshop, call and buy our book, register to get the book for free, or go and watch a video or order a DVD.

Whatever your offer is, this is where you have your sales pieces, your "about physical therapy" content and how you want that person to consume your offer.

Who To Send Your Newsletter To

Next we are going to cover the "Who"...

And it is quite simply this:

Any individual who has ever consumed an offer from you, you are going to want to continue to market to them.

It is much easier to provide value to your past patient list and promote to your past patient list than it is to the general public.

(At least IF the majority of the people that you have seen are satisfied with the quality of care that you have provided.)

If there has been some upset with you or your company and your past patient base, perhaps they are not going to respond.

I guess that is possible, but for the most part, people who have come into your clinic, who have done well, have received a service, have been fairly treated, have received your high quality of care are much more likely to return in the future.

So I would market to my past and present clients before I would go out and try to get people from the general public.

Special note - if you are a start-up, the one thing that I will hear is *"I will develop my patient newsletter later...once I already have patients to market to".*

I think that is an errant thought. It is a mistake in thinking.

The thing that you want to have right away is a system in place so once you get that first patient through, that they are communicated with forever and ever... An instant long-term relationship is developed and they receive a patient newsletter for the rest of their years.

When Should I Send a Newsletter Out?

The next thing I want to cover is when or how often you can mail your newsletter...

Through testing, we have found anywhere from 4 to 6 weeks works best. If we go more often than every 4 weeks (this is for direct mail), we lose effectiveness.

If we go longer than 6 weeks, we lose effectiveness.

So for the sake of our marketing calendar here at Madden Physical Therapy, we mail out a patient newsletter on a monthly basis.

Email or Snail Mail?

The next thing we will look at is where... or another way to think about it is "Media".

So what type of media do we use in promoting our patient newsletter?

Another common mistake that I see private practice owners make is they email their entire patient newsletter.

I know e-zines were absolutely a raging fad in the late 2000's, but more recently, just consider... would you ever read a full newsletter that was emailed to you?

Likely not.

The way that email is set up it is much more of a quick hit.

Effective email is one or two sentences and that's about it.

What we have found that works best here at Madden Physical Therapy is we send out a direct mail piece that is a printed patient newsletter mailed to over 7,700 past patients on a monthly basis.

Then we supplement that with an email to that past patient list as well that says, *"Hey, did you see this?"*

We call out one or two specific things...It's smaller. It's personal. It's a non-branded email (which we will talk about here later as well).

Those are the 2 types of media that we have found have worked best.

(So YES, it is snail mail and email combined.)

...BUT I've Never Put a Newsletter Together Before...

The last one that we will cover here is the "How."

Rather than you designing your newsletter in-house, which is the mistake I made in the beginning...

(When I started doing patient newsletters early in my private practice career, I would design them on Microsoft Publisher myself.)

And wasted hours upon hours creating them.

Then we would print them in-house on this ugly green paper and fold them ourselves...then mail them out.

What I learned was that was a huge waste of time and money.

What I have now learned to do is work with a good designer and printer. It's wise to have a printer that can accept the 3 components that we have already covered in Word format with one or two pictures that you supply.

The printer inputs our content into our standard newsletter template and they handle the mailing out as well.

I can tell you just from present pricing that you can have that done a lot more affordably than what most practice owners believe...

Do a little due diligence with finding a printer.

If you want a personal recommendation or a review, send me an email at **chad@breakthroughptmarketing.com** and I can give you the present printers that we are working with.

Want in to dig deeper into creating a
Killer Patient Newsletter System for your Private Practice?

You can apply for the next Killer Marketing Training class...

Join us at **www.breakthroughptmarketing.com/apply**

Chapter 9

Phase III - Physician Newsletters

Understanding How the Game of Doctor Referrals Has Changed

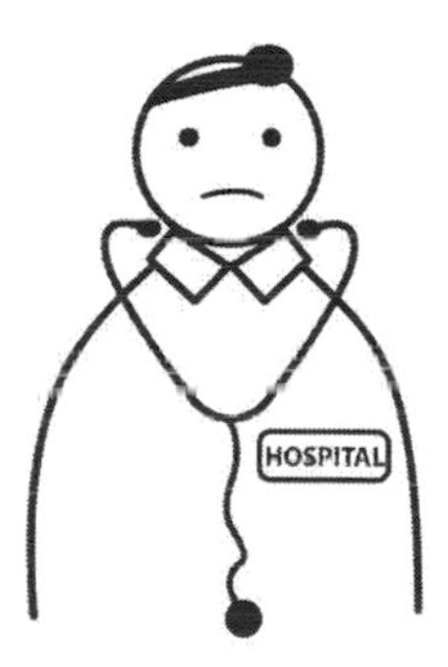

When I first opened up my private practice back in 2003, the name of the game, very much, was to get referrals from physicians.

Over the years, that has dramatically changed for a couple of reasons...

Direct Access...

As of this writing, we have Direct Access or quasi-Direct Access in 49 of the 50 states.

What that has allowed us to do is attract people from the general public.

Digging back into my exact numbers for you...back in 2007 we hit an all-time high of 154 physician referrals in one month.

That has declined by nearly 80% to the point now where we are averaging about 30 referrals a month from physicians.

Yet, again, we are busier than we were back in 2007.

So we are busier...have more income and are more profitable than ever before...resulting in significantly more stability as a private practice and business.

I want to show to you how we look at it now and how the game has changed.

The old game was *"We need referrals from doctors to survive."*

With POPTS practices, Direct Access, and with hospitals buying up and employing physicians... that game has changed.

Now the game is **we just want the family physicians and other clinicians in our area to keep the door open and not block access to care.**

For example, let's say that I host a workshop and a hypothetical patient named "Mary" comes through. In Pennsylvania, we can evaluate and treat without a physician referral for 30 days.

So let's say at the end of the 30 days, Mary needs to continue her plan of care.

We just simply want the physician to sign off on that plan of care extension.

***The nice thing is that the physician does not "get in trouble" for making the referral if they are just simply signing a plan of care.

The patient originated the referral. They guided their own care. They were involved in their own decision making and they were empowered.

So the physician doesn't get in trouble for that (at least with the hospital systems in my area).

The new game is: we just want the physician to keep the door open and allow those patients to continue their care with us.

Let me show you exactly how we have done that...

Who Do We Market To?

You'll want to market to MDs, DOs, family physicians, urgent care, orthopedic specialists, neurologists, OB/GYNs, urologists, podiatrists, dentists, nurse practitioners, PACs, midwives, doulas and any other licensed clinician in your state who could potentially refer a patient to you.

And yes, for some owners that I have worked with, that includes chiropractors, personal trainers and massage therapists as well.

The Two Types of Referral Sources

When we are talking about all of the clinicians in your area who could potentially make a referral to you, there are two types.

(I see a lot of owners make a mistake in terms of catering to the wrong type of referral source at least in my viewpoint and from my experience.)

Type #1 is the clinician who is thinking, *"What is in it for me?"*

This is the clinician who is looking for some sort of kickback...even though it may be unethical or illegal.

Perhaps they want to charge a lot of rent or a higher than fair market value for leasing space in exchange for the referrals (that is if you are renting from them)...

Perhaps they want some sort of nice dinner or some sort of special gift or acknowledgement that goes above and beyond what is normal with regards to the Stark Law and other healthcare laws which limit that.

So that's Type #1.

Type #2 is the clinician who simply value the high quality of care you provide.

They really care about their patients...they're going to make referrals for the right reasons.

That, to me, is the type of physician that we want to work with.

I have seen both...

You likely have as well.

Type #1 is fickle and flaky. They will chase whatever prize that awaits their referral. I would highly advise you NOT to play their game...it's too unstable...and provides zero foundation for you to build your private practice.

What has worked for me...and other private practice owners...is finding physicians who are referring to us for the right reasons.

So How Do You Find Clinicians Who Will Refer to You for the Right Reasons?

The biggest mistake that I see is (going back to that Market–Message–Media Match) most owners make the mistake of mailing the same exact newsletter to both patients and referral sources...

That's a HUGE error...

Let me just give you one big reason why this is such a big mistake...and the importance of you being aware of this AND avoiding it:

Language.

The way that you and I as Physical Therapists talk with referral sources is significantly different than the way we talk with patients.

Why? Well most physicians have 8 or more years of college and med school education...the language that they speak is significantly different than the lay public who we are most often treating.

The average reading level and writing level of our general patient base is roughly on a 5th grade level.

That's why the construction and the creation and execution of our patient newsletter is significantly different (with emphasis on more of the compelling personal interest story) than it is with our referral source base or our physician base.

To try to "kill two birds with one stone" here...and mail the same marketing piece to both Target Markets is a huge mistake.

We want two different newsletters going out.

Chapter 9

The #1 Single Biggest Advantage of a Physician Newsletter

When I opened and I first started in private practice, I had no idea how to market Madden PT.

I knew that I needed physician referrals because in Pennsylvania, we didn't have Direct Access yet.

So what I ended up doing was just going out and doing a ton of lunches.

In the first 4 months that I was open, I did 37 physician lunches.

Over time, what I learned is there is a much better way to do it...in terms of efficiency...both with regards to time and money.

So consider the average physician lunch...if there are 3 physicians and a physician's assistant in a practice and let's say that they have 20 total staff, to provide lunch in that case it's going to cost anywhere from $100 to $150.

The cost of mailing 150 referral sources is about $150.

So significantly more efficient.

I can get a lot more touches out there and can communicate in a much more effective way.

And what is going to happen is if I have a well-constructed physician newsletter that meets the criteria for the Market-Message-Media Match, then we're going to begin getting referrals for all of the right reasons.

We are going to attract the right type of physician with the goal of creating a long term professional referral relationship.

What Do We Put In The Newsletter?

I got this information from actual research of referral sources here in my area of Central Pennsylvania.

Back in 2005, we did a herniated disc survey...and wanted to know what percentage of physicians in our area believed that a herniated disc could heal, at least per MRI, with conservative treatment...with physical therapy.

What we found is 78% of the referral sources in our area agree that this was possible (or responded to the survey that healing a herniated disc with therapy was possible).

So really, really promising...good news for us in conservative care.

We dove a little bit deeper and asked the follow-up question: *"Where did you get this information? What journals are you reading?"*

We had a pretty comprehensive list of answers...of actual journals the local referral sources we're reading...

What I realized is that physicians and referral sources don't really consider physical therapy journals to be peer-reviewed research.

This is a really big deal because often what I see in physician newsletters (when they're different from the patient newsletters) is a lot of owners will include research that is physical therapy-based or published in physical therapy journals such as *JOSPT...JMMT* or...*The Physical Therapy Journal.*

We don't want to do that...because physicians don't read those journals AND they rarely consider them "peer reviewed"...

What we found is that the top 3 journals read by all physicians in our area were *JAMA (Journal of the American Medical Association),The Family Physician Journal and The New England Journal of Medicine.*

So what we began doing was anytime that we would reference some sort of physical therapy knowledge in our newsletter or in a luncheon or that we would reference a physical therapy journal article, we always cited a corresponding bit of research in a peer-reviewed journal as considered by the referral source...to back up the PT research.

(For example, I know one of the hallmark studies of the lumbopelvic Grade V mobilization or manipulation was first published in the *Annals of Internal Medicine*, so we will frequently reference that rather than the *JMMT* or *JOSPT* corresponding articles.)

So that is the research that goes into the physician newsletters as we have found it to work best.

The other costly mistake that I see is this:

Physicians don't really know what physical therapy certifications are and what they mean.

I'll give you an example of an actual Physical Therapist that I interviewed. To protect his identity...I'll refer to him as "Ernie."

Ernie came in to interview for a PT position and had an OCS.

He had just taken his test, passed his examination, had this designation on his CV. He really wanted to promote and market to the world that he had an OCS.

He asserted in the interview his belief that the majority of potential patients AND nearly every referral source knew what the OCS was, what it stood for...and how this designated the superior quality of care he delivered.

I challenged him with this question and it was from experience...

I said, *"That's great. We have other therapists who have the OCS. How many physicians in our area out of 400 do you think know what an 'OCS' is?"*

His response was, *"Nearly all of them."*

I said, *"I challenge you to name one...and I'll call them right now..."*

The interview did not go well, as you can imagine, but I said, *"I really want you to go out and just find me one physician who understands what the OCS is."*

I knew the majority of physicians do not value physical therapy certifications... they only value whether the patient comes back and says, *"I did great"* or *"Why did you send me to that PT?"*

That is what the physician is looking for out of their referral...

That the patient gets a positive result...

OR they complain.

They don't care or understand beyond that.

It's the patient result or the patient outcome...no complaints coming back to them.

That's what they are looking for.

Needless to say, I never heard back from "Ernie" again.

(Although when we ended up hiring another Physical Therapist..."Ernie" did call me to berate me that he thought the job would be his...)

Nonetheless it's unfortunate...but it's something that we learn in PT school: If we have a lot of letters after our name or a lot of designations... somehow that means that our value to the marketplace is higher.

It doesn't necessarily correlate that way.

(Realize that belief and mantra mentioned above originates with educators... NOT your potential patients or referral sources.)

If you are in private practice and you agree with the above viewpoint... and you find yourself thinking you need more clinical education when the road gets rocky in Private Practice PT...I urge you to look at that and get it resolved...because it's going to be tough to move forward and be successful if you believe that the number of letters after your name directly correlates to the number of new patients that are being referred to you...or the number your past patients that are coming back to you.

Putting it Together

Construction of the monthly physician newsletter has two parts.

The first part is going to be the research that we have already talked about.

You are pulling research from what physicians view as peer-reviewed journals.

The second part is you are going to tie it into a success story of how you are applying that research in your physical therapy practice and how you are getting results.

For example, if you choose that *Annals of Internal Medicine* piece of research on the lumbopelvic manipulation...your success story on the back of the newsletter... you're going to talk specifically about a patient that you applied that with and how well they did.

"Here is what this patient looked like on Day 1 when they came in for their eval."

In there, we talk about their objective and subjective measures (obviously with their permission).

Then, "Here's what life was like after physical therapy" including just one or two lines from the testimonial. Do not use the entire testimonial.

So part one is research.

Part two is a success story applying that research.

I don't want to spend too much time on the physician newsletter, because for most of us, we are trying to transition away from relying on physician referrals...

But just to give you an idea that you can still do something that is very simple to execute with a very low time and cost commitment.

Again, you can get your message out there and leave the door open for your referral sources.

Want to Take This a Step Further AND Build The Same Marketing Systems I Use Here At Madden PT?

You'll get access to the exact Physician Newsletters we create and use here at Madden PT PLUS training for you and your staff to build the same exact system...

Apply for the Next Killer Marketing Training by going to:
www.breakthroughptmarketing.com/apply

Chapter 10

Phase IV – Hosting Killer Workshops

Per Vision 2020 that the APTA released a number years ago...there's a big PT goal of having Direct Access in all 50 states and therapists being the clinicians of choice by the year 2020.

When we achieved that (at least in the majority of the states)...we made a major error as Private Practice PTs...

And the mistake is: **Direct Access is a destination for Physical Therapists.**

It's NOT a destination for our patients.

It's not what they need or want.

So the common error...the way that you will see this manifested is in private practice owners advertising their physical therapy services...they'll almost always include the actual term "Direct Access".

BUT "Direct Access" doesn't mean anything to the patient.

The private practice owners who are a little more advanced in their marketing will say something along the lines of, "You can now see a Physical Therapist without a doctor referral."

That's a little better... but frankly there is a much better way where we can provide value using the aforementioned principles of content marketing and direct response marketing that attracts the patient first (and that Direct Access just happens to be a little solution to a very small hurdle to access to care).

If you don't believe me or are having trouble understanding this, consider the example of pharmaceutical companies...which seem to be wildly successful and profitable. And in every single pharmaceutical that is ever sold legally (whether it is cash pay or insurance reimbursed)...it's done so with a physician referral.

Just think of what pharmaceutical companies have done with direct response marketing and how they have blown up over the last 15 years.

In private practice PT, if we are looking to do some sort of lead generation where we have people from the general public raising their hands and coming in to our clinics via Direct Access, we want to have a very significant offer that can come in one of three forms...

3 Forms of Content Marketing:

1. **Product**
2. **Service**
3. **Information**

This is known to high-end marketers as "Lead Generation".

What we are basically doing is having people from the general public raise their hands saying, *"Yes, I'm interested in that* (your product, service or information)."

What that allows us to do is give the potential client something for free in exchange for the ability to have ongoing communication with that potential client.

So if you have ever gone to a squeeze page and you entered in your name and email address in exchange for a free report or a free video or similar... you have gone through this process of Lead Generation yourself.

Now we want to take those same principles and apply it to your private practice so that people are raising their hands and coming into your private practice.

Of the 3 options to use for Lead Generation listed above...I'm the biggest fan of using **information.**

I think potential patients from the general public who are consumers of information make a much better patient on the back end.

They are more likely to respect you and respect your physical therapy knowledge and expertise and view you as an A.C.E. - Authority, Celebrity and Expert.

What I have found to work best is hosting a workshop where we invite people from the general public who have raised their hand and said, *"Yes, I have back pain or sciatica and I want to come in and learn more about that."*

I do not offer a free screen as Lead Generation upfront.

(Free Screenings, Discovery Visits, and Discovery Sessions are all forms of using a Service as Lead Generation).

In my experience, it doesn't work as well as workshops in ads.

I don't see a lot of people consuming it compared to information.

Again, this is referring to specifically offering free screenings to the general public.

I see a lot of chiropractors do it and a lot of private practice PT owners do it...

And you're more original than that...

To me, testing it here in my market in Central Pennsylvania, I have just found that it does not work nearly as well as hosting a workshop.

3 Steps to Hosting a Successful Workshop

If we are going to host a workshop and commit to it, we have to have goals.

Goal #1 is we want to get butts in seats. (Fill the room)

Goal #2 is we want to convert the people in the seats over to an exam.

Goal #3 is we want to convert those who attend the exam to a full plan of care.

How do we do that?

First...get butts in seats.

I don't know if you have seen it or not, but on Facebook, LinkedIn, almost everywhere on the internet and even in *Impact Magazine*, we have had an offer to share the exact copy that I use to advertise my workshops.

This works in two types of media in particular - which are postcards and print ads.

It can also work on Facebook, email copy, social media, etc.

For my private practice and for others now all over the U.S., they found the most success in postcards and print ads.

Here at the end of this chapter, we will be sharing a story with you from Lee Sowerbutts and his brother, Scott...they thought outside the box and used the same exact copy that I am willing to share with you and they hosted a workshop at a gym...and had unbelievable results for less than $6...

I'll share that story with you at the end of the chapter.

If you are interested in using the same exact print as that I use, you can go through breakthroughptmarketing.com/workshop

(When you go and register there...I'll give you an offer at the end to get and use the same exact copy that I am using in my postcards and print ads to advertise for my workshop.)

The second step is we want to convert those that actually attend over to an examination.

How do we do that?

I don't have the time to go into it right here within the pages of this book, but basically there are a few things that you can do in your workshop...in your presentation...that are really going to help you convert people to sign up.

First, you'll want to do some sort of demonstration.

What I do in the very beginning of the workshop, I say, "This workshop is going to be interactive."

I have everybody stand up, bend forward, bend backward, side to side.

Then I look for somebody with pain.

I ask them to volunteer.

I bring them up to the front of the room.

I give myself about 5 minutes to create some sort of meaningful and visual change.

(Really what I am looking for is for them to say, *"Wow, I do feel a lot better."*)

Then demonstrate the change...for example, if the volunteer is in obvious pain with extension before my 5 minute treatment...I'll retest after the treatment...looking to show the volunteer AND the audience that PT can produce results.

So I do that first...

Talking at Your Audience Versus Interacting With Your Audience

The average workshop that I have seen recorded by other practice owners (before they go through the Killer Workshop Training) will include no demonstration at all. It usually involves a lot...nearly 100%...of the Physical Therapist talking at their audience.

I have found that that does not work. (There's one exception to this...I've worked with one owner who does no demonstration...yet maintains nearly 80% conversion to an appointment.)

What I have found that works much better than talking at the audience...is if the workshop is interactive.

Along those lines, we also provide a worksheet... so every member of the audience has a pen and the worksheet...they complete the worksheet as I go throughout my presentation.

(This prevents yawning, day dreaming...or worse, falling asleep!)

I have 3 big points that I am covering in the workshop and each one of those leads the person closer to scheduling an appointment.

That's where we are going...we're delivering a ton of value...providing lots of valuable information...with the goal of the workshop attendee scheduling an appointment.

At the end, I have a big close (and you should too...when I was on Paul Wright's podcast...he made the super wise recommendation that this is the most important part of the workshop...and the one you should practice the most...and he's 100% right). The close sounds something like this:

"That concludes the workshop. I don't normally offer free screenings to the general public, but since you are here and you have raised your hand, you called to register, you showed up here to the Back Pain and Sciatica Workshop, you have listened, you've been interactive, you've filled out your worksheet and you have seen what this type of natural treatment can do for you and you have indicated that you want to get back to normal... here is my offer to you. I'm just going to do this today. If you schedule an appointment before you leave, I'll offer you a free screening. And what you are going to get from that free screening are two things:

1. *You are going to know the exact cause of your back pain and sciatica.*
2. *You are going to know what successful treatment - specific for the cause of your back pain and sciatica - looks like."*

What I will do from there is if we have a large group, I will dismiss them in order of severity.

"Who has severe pain and needs to be seen right now?"

Those people raise their hand.

"Ok, you can go and schedule."

What we want to do is have an orderly format where we are dismissing people from the room and I am hanging around answering questions...

Those people that need to be seen the most, can go and schedule right away.

A big error that I see is a lot of presenters will not practice their close.

It is probably the most important part of the entire presentation.

Converting to a Full Plan of Care

The third step is converting those people to a full plan of care once they are in the examination.

For that we use a system called **The 7 Step Killer Exam** that we covered in Phase I of the Killer Marketing Secrets.

I want to share the story of Lee and Scott Sowerbutts with you of and how they are absolutely crushing it with Killer Workshops:

"It's difficult to put an exact dollar amount on what I've learned over the past year. We are putting into place new systems, and refining old ones. Systems that will reap benefits in the future. As far as marketing goes, we now have a specific plan that someone else (Chad) has refined. I look at this as a long term investment in our business. Obviously, none of us want to throw money at something that doesn't help the bottom line. I have seen enough of a return on investment with the strategies we have implemented to "stick around". I'm not sure if Chad has given y'all the y=x^n^ speech, but we all can't flip a switch and have tons of new patients just walk in the door. It takes a plan, hard work and consistency. We haven't implemented all the information, strategies, and ideas taught immediately. That would be

overwhelming! Early on there were times I felt like my head was spinning. But when we have strategically pulled the trigger on a process, the results have been amazing.

Here's one example that we implemented...the workshop. My workshop story...

So just to give you a little context, I am a physical therapist in Hot Springs, Arkansas. I own two clinics that are approximately 20 miles from each other. We opened the second clinic in Hot Springs Village in September 2014. It's a gated community of approximately 10,000 residents. Most of the residents are retired and very active. Just to give you an idea of how active they are, the community has ten 18-hole golf courses, five lakes, a beautiful tennis complex and a huge fitness natatorium.

OK, so back to the workshop... I was attending a recreational expo to help promote our clinic and the director of the fitness center approached me about teaming up with them to do some sort of event. At that time, I was currently going through the Killer Marketing 2.0 course and was not in a position to really add an additional time commitment. We were implementing Chad's strategies and trying to cultivate a culture where our past patients were sharing their experiences with their friends and family about our services. Both clinics continue to grow steadily. Fast forward to October. I decided it was time to implement the workshop strategy Chad had discussed in the "24 Months to All Star" program. I reached out to the fitness director and decided to target the first Saturday in November to host a workshop on back pain and sciatica. We discussed how we wanted to advertise/market the workshop. We came up with the idea of distributing canary yellow pamphlets using the exact copy that Chad had given us in his workshop module. We provided the fitness director with an email (again using the copy that Chad had provided for us) and she sent it to the community.

The e-blast was sent out Wednesday night and by noon the following day we already had 25 people register for the workshop (Scott said we've struck a "nerve" with this workshop thing). We decided to limit our registration at 50 attendees and once we were full immediately made plans for a second workshop in December.

So here are the numbers of the November workshop...we had 50 registrants with 44 attendees with 21 scheduling the free screen. For the December

workshop we had 41 register 25 attended with 14 scheduling the free screen. So you're probably wondering how this impacted our numbers for November and December.

For the month of November, we had 33 referrals (97001s) @ our HSV clinic with our previous record being 18.

Combining both clinics, we set a new record of 68 referrals for the month of November with our previous record being 53.

Our patient visit numbers for the HSV clinic for the month of December increased from around 150/month to a record of 262 actual patient visits. We also set a record in December for total patient visits for both clinics at 630.

OK... so now for the good stuff! You're probably wondering how much we spent on marketing? We bought 500 sheets of canary yellow multipurpose color paper at a cost of $9.49. We took 50 sheets of that paper and printed Chad's exact copy. We took the 50 printed sheets to the Coronado Fitness Center & left them near the check-in desk. Quick math...paper costs were $0.019/sheet & $0.03/sheet ink cost for a total cost of $2.45... And we still have about 25 remaining sheets :)"

– **Lee Sowerbutts,** Arkansas

Chapter 11

How PTs Can Really Get Patients from the Internet

Internet Marketing taught by Carl Mattiola
(who is NOT a PT...but an actual, real-life Internet Marketer)

SECTION 1 - INTRODUCTION

The Biggest Challenge in PT Internet Marketing

I was checking my email the other day and I heard from a practice owner who was really frustrated...

He was asking me a question because he had invested quite a bit of money into some social media and online advertising.

He wasn't sure what his return was on that.

He wasn't actually sure where his patients were coming from or if he was even getting a return at all.

He called me...let's name him "Mike".

Mike said, *"Hey, Carl, I don't know exactly, I have invested all of this money in this social media company and this online marketing company that did my website, but I don't really know if I'm getting patients from there. Sometimes people say it is the website. Sometimes they don't. But I don't actually know what is working and what is not and where people are coming from. Is there a way to track that?"*

I said, *"Mike, yeah, there should be."*

To those of you reading this, I wonder if that resonates with you?

If you've spent money marketing your practice on the internet before, I bet it does. When it comes to internet marketing, this is probably what I hear most frequently from people in private practice physical therapy.

It is the big challenge that I hear – *"I don't even know if it is working or if it is not."*

You probably hear about the internet, social media, and how you're now living in a time where you can reach an audience instantly for cheaper than ever possible...

At some point you might have gotten excited about this opportunity and have blindly spent money with a company who had lots of promises...only to see that months later...you have no idea if you are getting results or not.

Let me tell you something most crappy, lazy, local marketing companies out there try to hide...

Internet marketing is the easiest marketing to measure...and if you're doing it right...you should know your exact return on investment and exactly how many patients you're getting from it each month.

It's likely to give you your highest ROI of any marketing you do and open you up to all the cool opportunities that the internet provides: instant access to your audience for cheap, incredible tracking and accountability, laser-focused targeting, and automation that help you convert traffic, into leads, into workshop registrations, into free screens, into full POCs, additional cash-pay services that maximize profits, and your return path (past patients coming back or past patients referring friends).

So in this chapter, I'm going to tell you how you can actually benefit from the internet using real stories of tested tactics:

- How you can do things like we have been able to do, send a single email campaign with a little automation that can generate 20 patients a month from a 1,000 person email list.
- Or how you can get 30 registrations for a back pain workshop in a week from Facebook...
- How you can partner with a local gym to get 21 new patients for a total cost of $1.97.
- And for those who want to get hardcore... How you can build an automatic patient machine using automation that converts traffic, into leads, into uber-motivated prospects of your services...into patients that complete their full plan of care...buy profit maximizing cash-based services...and then refer their family and friends...with automation... I've made this a reality for several practice owners already...and you can use it too.

That is what I'm going to explain to you in this chapter.

I promise you, if you pay attention to this and you implement it, you are going to get results.

Anybody who has done this in our group so far, that has used it, has gotten tremendous results and done it right and stuck with it.

I'm excited for you and you should be, too.

SECTION 2 - FUNDAMENTALS

Understanding The Media Internet

What I'm about to tell you is the single most important thing to get right in online marketing (and ALL marketing).

This information is TIMELESS...

As different trends rise and fall throughout time (Facebook, Twitter, email, Pintrest, Instagram)... this will remain true...

Market-Message-Media Match

Just like Chad explained in an earlier chapter about the Market-Message-Media Match formula, it applies to any type of marketing and it is very important to pay attention to it on the internet as well.

Let me explain in a quick story...

At the BPTM Killer Marketing Bootcamp I had this practice owner say to me, *"Hey, I'm sending all of these emails, every month. I'm getting no response."*

So I asked him to show me the email...

What he showed me was an email with the subject (I'm going to make up a name here because I didn't ask to share this), *"Forest Physical Therapy Monthly Announcement".*

When you opened it up, it was this big massively designed email.

It looked kind of like a flyer or a full-on webpage.

A blue background color, big white font, lots of pictures, and worst of all, no real call to action.

And I have to admit... This is the type of email I see from most practice owners and I am not sure why or how this trend started... Maybe it's because people think that when they make something look "flashy" more will read it... Maybe it's because other marketing companies try to sell you services that put this nonsense together... Or maybe it's because your email software has the features...

Either way... The problem with this type of email will not get opened...will not get read...and certainly will not get you any patients...

Think about it... Can you tell me anytime that you have actually opened an email that had an announcement name like that and then you have actually read it and were consuming an email where it looked like a flyer? I'd be pretty surprised.

Instead, here's how you have to solve the problem...look at the media (in this case email) and think about how you use it.

What kinds of emails do you open?

There are only 2 answers that come up the most (email me at **carl@breakthroughptmarketing.com** if you have another).

1) Emails from friends, colleagues, or coworkers
2) Emails that give you value (teach you something, make you laugh, make you feel good)

All other emails usually get ignored... And here's why... You're competing with LOTS of other emails for attention.

Email (and the internet in general) is great because you have instant access to a whole bunch of markets, but the downside is you are competing with tons of people and tons of emails and tons of Facebook posts and tons of stuff happening all over the place.

When you send an email, you are competing with all of that. People have a short attention span when in their inbox (and this happens to be true for most media on the internet).

Think about it. What does your inbox look like?

If you're like most people, it's filled with a ton of new email everyday. So many, that it's probably impossible for you to open and read every one...

When you send emails to past patients, you are dealing with the same problem.

It's this that makes the message (in particular the email subject) even more important than most other media.

If I were to ask you if you could remember one email subject that you got in the last two days, I'd be really surprised if you could remember.

I know that I can't remember any of them myself and this is something that I do for a living...I pay attention to those things.

The reason is because you get so many.

If I asked you how much time you spend when you look at each email in your inbox, you would probably tell me a fraction of a second.

I know that is how much time I give it.

And in that fraction of a second, you are making a decision to throw it out or ignore it or open it.

The key here is to understand what are the emails that you are going to open and what are the emails that you are going to throw away?

The same is going to be true pretty much for your patients.

For example...

What email are you more likely to open?

Subject A: ABC Company Newsletter

Subject B: Quick question for you...

Definitely B right?

So the next time you write an email, look in your own inbox for emails from friends or from people who send you valuable stuff. Take a look at what you open.

Model that for your next email.

So when you are creating any advertising piece for the internet (Emails, Facebook Posts, Tweets) you need to think about the internet as a media first.

Do not get caught up in the hype of the tactics...

And do not forget about Market-Message-Media Match.

If you get this right, you'll do great.

In the next section, I'm going to tell you the one approach that always works in marketing.

This is a truth that holds true no matter what the Market, Media, or Message...

SECTION 3 - FUNDAMENTALS - GIVE VALUE

Last year, I paid $20,000 to go to a 2 day training by Frank Kern (a very successful teacher of internet marketing).

Some people think Frank's methods can come across as overbearing at times, but that's because he knows his market (internet marketers) who appreciate the weird and sometimes aggressive messages...

Anyway, at the training, one thing that stuck out from the full day Frank taught on psychology was this...

"If you remember anything I've told you today, give tons of value and you'll do great. Value trumps all other tactics."

Neil Patel, who's known to be another one of the best marketers alive right now, his main piece of advice for people: Create one piece of valuable content everyday.

Seth Godin...same thing...

Seeing the trend here?

If you want to succeed in business and especially on the internet, you must give massive value upfront.

Frank Kern says the amount of customers you have and money you make is directly proportional to 2 things:

1. The amount of offers you make.
2. And the amount of goodwill you have with your audience.

Herein lies the problem...

You can't make offers all the time because it will seem spammy and salesy.

You don't want to feel slimy by sending an email out saying, "Hey, come in for a visit."

That doesn't work.

What happens if you send too many offers, people just start to ignore your message like we talked about in the previous section.

It also feels crappy to be sending that kind of message all the time, right?

But we must have a call to action, and we must make an offer if we want to convert the general public into followers, into email subscribers, into workshop attendees, and finally into a full plan of care...all the way up the funnel.

So how can we solve that?

It's actually pretty simple (and it feels really good at the same time).

What if we could always give value and always make offers at the same time?

If we are always giving value to the market and are always giving them what they want...and the offer you're making has value in and of itself...then you can make as many offers as you want and get as many leads, and patients as you want.

For example, somebody that has back pain, what might be useful to them is the "Top 3 Exercises to Cure Your Back Pain" or a "self-test to diagnosis what is causing your back pain". (Those are just a couple of examples.)

What if we always led with value and giving something good to people?

Then on the back end, only after someone consumes the goodwill content we made an offer related to that content that gives the consumer more value?

That does two things for us...

1. It allows us to be able to give value to the market.

So you are giving value and then...

2. You are making an offer only to the people who are interested in what you are giving away.

Here's a quick example using real email that I've used for some of our high end clients at BPTM...one that got 22 patients by sending 2 emails to a list of about 1200 past patients.

The email subject was (and you can copy it - that is totally fine) : *"Only open if you have back pain..."*

It may seem counterintuitive that you are pushing some people away... but you are...and you are valuing people's time and they agree with that.

And if the email is something of value to people with back pain, those are the only people that matter to be reading this message.

What is really cool about that is if they open that email, they probably have back pain or they know somebody who does.

Then inside that email, you might say:

> *Hey John - Have something really cool to share with you.*
>
> *It's a new blog post called "The Top 3 Exercises for Lower Back Pain".*
>
> *If you have any lower back pain, these exercises could help you get relief in as little as 5 minutes.*
>
> *Click here to read it.*
>
> *To Your Health,*
> *Carl*
>
> *PS - Since you read this email, you probably either have back pain or know someone who does. So please reply to this email and let me know if there is any way I can help :)*

What does that do?

First, the subject identifies the right people who will get value from this email, so it gets opened by the right people. If John opens the email, he likely either has some back pain or knows someone who does.

Next, it's in plain text and is personal (the types of emails people read).

Then it has 2 calls to action (CTAs).

The first is to click to see the exercises in the blog post, which offers value for John.

Inside the post itself you'll actually have another call to action at the end. This way the reader will not get to the offer until they've already gotten a lot of value.

By the way, the offer should be related to the content you're giving.

In this case, the CTA would be something like, *"If you are experiencing back pain and you liked this post, then you might also like to come to our free back pain and sciatica workshop..."*

The next CTA is in the PS. It's simply a soft and personal offer to help this person (or their friend) with their back problem, by asking them specifically to reply.

Now there is one more advanced thing you can do to get an even better response out of this little email campaign, and it's what I did that got owners upwards of 20 patients each time they used it. That is by making another offer only to people who clicked the link using automation. More on this at the end of this chapter, but what we did was immediately after they click the link, we automatically send another email asking them how they're feeling and if they could use help.

So let's review what happened here.

We gave John value first. Then, only after giving him some value and treating him personally, we made a few offers (3 actually).

Last, everything we sent and every offer is trackable so you can see how many leads you got from each email (via email opens, link clicks, and email responses back).

And what about people who did not open this email? Well, no harm done.

We've excluded them and honored their time upfront by using a subject that tells them if this is worth their time or not.

If you market like this online, wrapping everything you do in value, you can make more offers, feel good about doing it, have a better relationship with your list (so less unsubscribes and more interaction), and get more patients in the process.

SECTION 4 - TRAFFIC - EMAIL

Now that you have 2 important fundamentals under your belt, we'll get into some of the tactics. In this section we are going to talk about traffic, and go into more detail on the most effective form of traffic I know of online that's worked the best for all the practices I've helped out (and honestly in all the businesses I've worked with outside of PT, too).

What is traffic?

Remember the patient funnel Chad talked about earlier in the book? Where you start with the general public, drive traffic to offers, then a lead magnet, tripwire, core service, cash and high end services, and return path...

The same thing exists online as it does offline. You're just using different media.

Now there are 3 types of traffic (this applies online and offline).

1) Hot Traffic - People who have already bought your services (your past patients).
2) Warm Traffic - People who know you (or know others who know you).
3) Cold Traffic - People who don't know you at all.

When marketing, it's always a good idea to go for the low hanging fruit first, and that is your HOT and WARM traffic (or your past and present patients and your followers).

If I were to give you one thing, one single thing to do to move forward with, the most effective tactic that I know is email marketing.

A lot of you are going to maybe just think about skipping this chapter because you have tried it and failed...

That is a mistake. It would be a huge mistake.

If you have an email list or you don't have an email list, either way, you are totally missing out if you are not doing this.

You are totally missing out if you are doing it because you most likely are not doing it properly.

The reason is you don't have the right message for this media.

Most people don't. Most people don't know how to do it.

Remember the story in Section 2 about the owner who was sending emails with "announcement" like subjects and brochure or flyer looking emails?

If that's what you've done in the past, try some of the new things I've showed you instead. I promise, it will make a difference.

Now I've already showed you the basics in the last few sections, so let's review them.

1) Write a personal or value-driven subject line (look to your own inbox for ideas based on what you click)

Here are some examples...

Let's start with "personal" because I believe those are the most opened emails and the best things that you can do.

First, who the email comes from should never be "Forest Physical Therapy" or the name of your business. It should always be your first name. So the from field should say "Jane" or "John".

Here's an example of a personal subject line that works well. "Hey, first name" or just "Hey" or "Quick question."

Why does this get opened?

Well, you see that and you see that maybe it comes from Mike, who runs Forest Physical Therapy, instead of just Forest Physical Therapy.

So on the left side of your Gmail or whatever email that you use or your iPhone or whatever phone that you're using, you see the person's name, Mike, instead of Forest Physical Therapy.

Then after that, you see that it says, "Hey, first name".

Let's say your name is Jen... it says, "Hey Jen".

What is the likelihood that you are going to click on that?

It is pretty likely because it is a pretty personal thing.

Look at the difference in how this looks in my inbox...

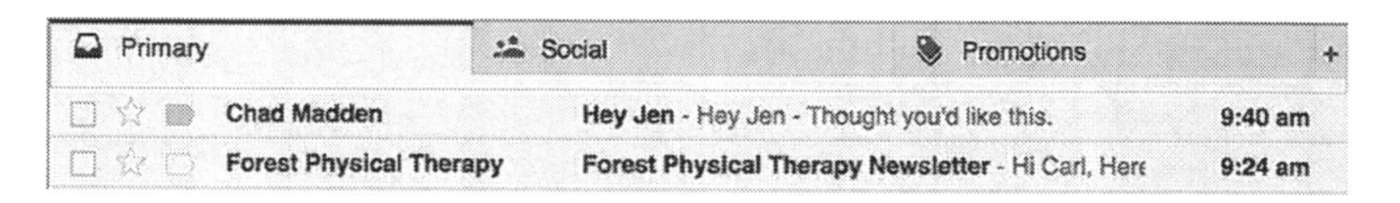

First one comes from "Chad Madden" a real person. Subject is personal and mentions your name.

Second one comes from a business name and has a subject that does not have much meaning.

Which do you open? Pretty obviously the first one right?

Another thing worth mentioning is you can use people's names in email subjects through mail merge in most email tools. Later in this section, I'll make some recommendations for you.

Using someone's name in the subject can boost your open rates.

So if you have something useful in the subject or something personal, it is going to get opened.

So, "Hey, first name" or "Quick question, first name" or just "Question for you..."

Experience shows these types of subjects get opened way more than anything else.

Now let's do an example using a value-driven or useful subject.

Do you know what a useful email subject is for somebody who is your target client?

So let's say that your target client is similar to Chad's... Maybe it is men and women over 55 with a higher income level who have back pain.

So what could be useful for those people? What are those people thinking and feeling?

Well, the first thing that you want to do is ask them... like what works well for them.

You can get some of our copy if you buy the postcard or print ad or the Back Pain and Sciatica Workshop.

What works?

"The Top 3 Exercises for Back Pain and Sciatica."

That would work well as far as a useful subject. Or the one I said before, "Only open if you have back pain."

Then you get the people to open the email.

Again, the email subject is the single most important thing about the email because if it doesn't get opened, if somebody doesn't open it, nothing is going to happen.

Once they open it, what do you want it to look like inside?

Like I mentioned about the Forest PT email, it looked like a big designed webpage.

That stuff doesn't work.

I will tell you why...

Because it is impersonal.

And honestly, it is harder to read.

You want it to look like an email that you send your friend.

Let's look at an example:

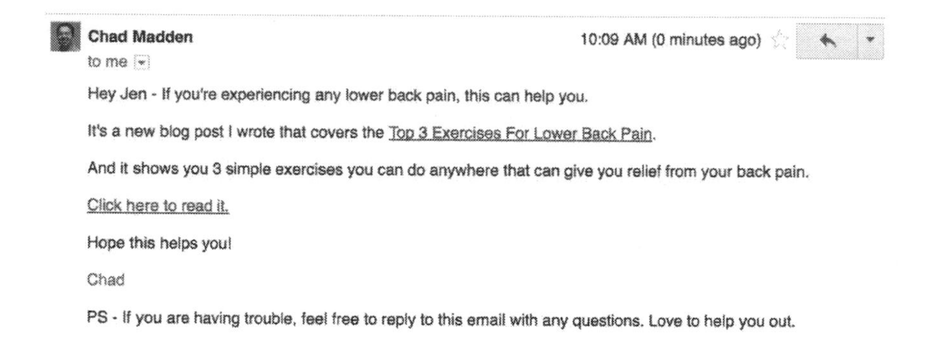

There is a lot of copywriting formats that you can follow, but here is the one that I like.

It is very simple... Here's the template:

"Hey First Name - I have something useful for you.

- What it is.
- What it will do for them.
- How they get it.
- Link to get it.
- Hope this helps you!

Your Name"

Let's examine this example.

Short personal greeting and personal copy.

Not super designed. Looks like it came from a friend.

Short sentences that are easy to read.

Clearly gives the reader the benefits they get.

Last, a clear call to action.

And bonus - a soft call to action in the PS to encourage interaction.

Email is a communication piece. It is used to talk back and forth. Treat it that way, and you'll see real results.

Okay now let me recommend a couple tools for email that I like.

1) Campaign Monitor (cheap, super simple)

2) Active Campaign (a little more expensive with basic automation capability)

3) Infusionsoft (By far the most expensive and most powerful in terms of automation. I don't recommend this to any practice owner unless you're going to hire someone to help you. More on automation later and how we help people with it).

All of these tools will allow you to send emails to your entire email list at once and use mail merge in order to personalize the email.

Now, since I have gone through that, I'm just going to give you one simple email you can use that works well for any business.

It is called the single question email.

So here is what you are going to do for your patient list.

You are going to get your patient list and you are going to sign up for one of those services - say Campaign Monitor.

And you are going to send an email just like this:

Subject: "Quick question" or ideally, "Quick question first name" (if you have names...)

Email body:

> "Hey Amy,
>
> Just doing a quick survey. Do you have back pain?
>
> Kindly reply to this email with your answer.
>
> Thanks :)
>
> Carl"

So you are going to send that email out to your whole list.

Not one at a time.

With the tools above, you can email one to many. You will only have to write it once. And with mail merge, it will handle everything. You just wait to see how many responses you get.

Now, when people respond it will be either yes or no.

Regardless of what they respond with, you win.

If they say yes, obviously you can try to have a conversation or call them right away and see if they are interested in anything or if there is any way that you can help them.

If they say, no, you can be like, "Ok great, do you know anybody who might have back pain?"

Because this could be a past patient of yours who got really good care... so they might reach out to somebody for you.

That is it. Seems too simple...

That's what I thought too. It's also how most owners felt when I showed this to them...

But for the few who listen and try it... They get TONs of emails back. Each one is a lead. Have a conversation and offer a screen if it makes sense. We've gotten people with lists of 1000 emails over 80 responses and more than 15 new full POCs as a result.

And you don't need 1000 people on your list. It will work with even 50 or so. You can send it to your friends and it will work, too.

I highly recommend that you check it out and do that.

If you do, email me at **carl@breakthroughptmarketing.com** with the results and what happened or if there are any questions.

If it did work for you and you want to learn more, just email me and let me know and I will put together a more extensive webinar on email and internet marketing for physical therapy practices based on all of the things that I have learned.

Now that you have the basics of email marketing. We're going to talk about getting cold traffic and building your email list through the media that we've seen working the best across the 100s of practices we help. Facebook.

SECTION 5 - TRAFFIC - FACEBOOK

I was out to dinner a few nights ago with Jen (my girlfriend) and her family.

Her mother, aunts, and uncles were there. All of them must be between 55 and 70 years old (guessing and hope this doesn't get me in trouble :)

Anyway, as I sat there eating, Jen and I noticed that every single one of them were on their iPhones at the same time.

What could be so captivating that they all wanted to be on their phones at dinner when they could be talking to one another?

I took a guess and I was right.

Every single one of them were on Facebook, looking at their newsfeed, checking out the comments people were putting up on the photos they just took earlier that night.

In this section, we're going to cover the best source of cold traffic for attracting new patients to Madden PT and our clients practices... And that is Facebook.

The reason I tell that story is a lot of people don't believe it's possible to have a profitable return using Facebook to market their private practice.

Most think their market is not on there. They think it's for kids.

Wrong.

They are on there, and you can put up targeted direct response content and advertisements to draw them into your patient funnel.

And guess what else...

Of all the sources of traffic we've tested for workshops, Facebook, when used properly, has provided the cheapest cost per plan of care.

Let me explain how.

First, on Facebook you have the ability to target Hot, Warm, and Cold traffic.

Again, let's start with Hot and Warm traffic first.

On Facebook, you have the ability to first and foremost market to your fans and people who follow you. And you can also get your past patients as part of your fan base pretty easily.

So that is the first "low hanging fruit" that you should tackle on Facebook is to get your past patients to be fans of your Facebook page.

To do that it is really simple...

If you have a list of your emails and phone numbers, you have the ability to upload that into Facebook and to use that as a custom audience (which is basically just a way of setting targets for Facebook ads).

Once you've uploaded that list to create an audience of your past patients, you have a nice hot audience to start with. You should also target people who like your page and their friends (more hot and warm traffic).

Then you can boost Facebook posts (costs about $20) to these highly targeted audiences.

I have helped a few practice owners in the Breakthrough PT Marketing program get that set up and they have gotten very good results from it...

10 or 20 registrations for workshops from that type of targeting alone just from their past patient base and fan base...

Next we should talk about what to put in your posts. The fundamentals you learned earlier hold true... lead with value and pay attention to the media, in this case, Facebook.

If you are doing a Facebook post, this is probably a good time for me to talk about the anatomy of a post.

When you are creating a post, it is made up of 4 things:

1. A headline
2. An image (or video)
3. Some body copy
4. Call to action

Now, when you are working in the media of Facebook, the #1 most important thing to have is a good image that is related to what you are doing, but is also going to attract people's attention - because on Facebook, people are exploring...

They are browsing.

They are scrolling the feed and the first thing that they are going to look at is the image.

The next thing that they are going to look at is the headline.

So if they have an image that attracts their attention, the next thing that they are going to look at is the headline.

Then, after they read the headline, if the headline is compelling, it will cause them to read the body or maybe just click right away (or do whatever it is that you want them to do).

When I am marketing, I like to look at what is what type of content my ideal prospect is consuming AND how they are consuming that content in that media.

So on Facebook, I can tell you that there really are a couple of good people that you can follow, a couple of good businesses that you can follow that have basically dominated Facebook the most recently.

It is really funny because it is these goofy posts that people are clicking on that they are super curious about... cute cats or about just different stories that you would be super curious about... stuff that you would see in The National Inquirer.

It is like the new version of that on Facebook.

These sites are called BuzzFeed and ViralNova and even the Huffington Post (which I would say is a little bit more like a normal news channel).

They make their money by putting up really good Facebook posts, getting people to like it and getting them to share it.

If you model after that when you are posting and you use really good curiosity and those types of images...

For example, something that might work on Facebook would be the headline, "My back was hurting so much I couldn't walk. You will never believe what happened when I..."

You are leaving a cliff hanger there.

That kind of thing works really well.

The other type of content people engage with on Facebook is content from their friends. So you should use a strategy similar to what we discussed in the email section. Make your posts look like a post your friends are sharing.

Take a look at what it looks like when your friends are sharing a post with you and mimic that.

Typically the post content looks like this:

"Friends who are ____ should check this out. It can help you..."

"If you're ___ you should see this..."

That type of thing... After that they share the link and people see and click because it looks as if it came from a person or a friend.

Now lets talk about images.

Experience has shown images of your target market work really well. So think about your ideal patients and what they look like... Images of people who look like this will work... Especially when the image is related to the content you're sharing... So say you put up a post for runners... An image of someone in your target market running could work quite well.

Other options to test are flat art (just Google that and you'll get an idea of what I mean). You can also add some text to the image as an extra headline, but the text can not take up more than 20% of the image.

For the headline, you want to deliver value. Think about the biggest pains or desires of your target market and use that in the headline. One simple formula I use often is "How To YAY without NAY".

Example: How To Heal Back Pain Permanently Without Medication, Injections, Or Surgery

Yay being a big benefit. And Nay being a big objection, pain, or fear.

If you go to **KillerMarketingSecretsBook.com/Resources** I'll also give you a list of my favorite headline formulas.

Now onto body copy and the CTA.

In the body of the post, like I said before, you'll want to elaborate further on the subject of what you are sharing. So here's what you should do. Be personal, dig into the pain they are having and the benefits they want to receive. Then make a call to action.

One thing to note... Make sure you are very careful to follow the Facebook guidelines for ad content. There are a lot of extra rules for people marketing services in Healthcare. So if you have an ad that is not being approved, it's likely because you are breaking some of Facebook's ad guidelines for Healthcare.

There are a lot of rules on Facebook against assuming somebody has pain when you are marketing to them.

The last and most powerful (but also most difficult step) is getting cold traffic.

This is where things can get really, really exciting for the PT market. I cannot come close to teaching you to run Facebook ads in one chapter of a book, so instead I simply want to show you what is possible.

First, hardly anyone is doing this. When you combine what I told you about before or when you combine squeeze pages (you'll hear about in next section) with cold traffic with Facebook using Facebook ads, it becomes a really powerful way to get Direct Access patients if you do it right... and as I mentioned before, Facebook ads provide the cheapest new cold traffic we know of.

The downside is it is very difficult to do. The rules are constantly changing.

With cold traffic, what is really cool with Facebook is it gives you, if you go into the ad manager, you are able to really target people in really specific ways... ways that you wouldn't believe that they have the ability to do.

You can start off with general things like age, sex, and zip code.

But Facebook can go way beyond this and even target by things like the company they work at, the different interests they have (CrossFit, yoga, running), and even their net worth (I know scary right?)...

I know this is totally creepy from a personal standpoint, but as a marketer of your practice, this is crazy awesome.

You can get into details like targeting woman between 30 and 35 who have recently bought baby products that live in selected zip codes.

You can target people who work at a company near you that has insurance you have a contract with and pays well.

You can even target people who have spent money on pain management, believe it or not, through different ways.

Lastly, you can even use something called retargeting and show ads to people who've visited your website in the past! This is done by putting some code on your site that tracks them.

Facebook is an amazing tool. Start small by putting some valuable posts with good clear CTAs up.

Then boost those posts.

And if you're really hard core and want to be able to turn on the faucet... look into running Facebook Ads to your local general public.

If you'd like to learn more about how to do it, go to **KillerMarketingSecretsBook.com/Resources** to attend my next free webinar on online marketing for PTs.

SECTION 6 - CONVERSION, WEBSITES, SQUEEZE PAGES, AND FOLLOW-UPS

So at this point you can drive some very targeted traffic from well written emails and Facebook post... But how the heck do we convert this traffic into prospective patients or leads?

And how do we keep track of what is working and what is not?

At this point, you've already learned some basic calls to action (CTAs) like email me or call this number.

Now you're going to learn about something much more powerful called Squeeze Pages.

A squeeze page is the most effective tool to deliver a lead magnet.

I'm talking a lot of jargon here, but I am assuming since you guys are reading this book, at this point you have already read Chad's chapter on the patient funnel.

What it looks like is it starts with traffic... and on the internet, it works the same way.

Your traffic could be coming from email.

Your traffic could be coming from the general public from Facebook.

It could be coming from your Facebook fans.

It could be coming from your website (Google, Bing, Yahoo, etc...)

It could be coming from social media, like review sites like Yelp.

It could be coming from all of these places, but then how do you collect them?

And what do they do?

And how do you collect their contact information so you can call them, build your email list, and start a relationship?

The best way is to offer a lead magnet in exchange for a prospective patients contact information via a squeeze page.

Usually this is a free offer for information like a report, video, or presentation, but it can sometimes be a paid offer as well.

In some cases, it could even be something physical, like a lacrosse ball or exercise bands (anything related to the PT service you offer that would attract your ideal client).

What we have found to work best is information in the form of reports or presentations or videos about the subject that your target patient wants to learn and/or is feeling.

So what is a squeeze page?

A squeeze page is a special kind of webpage, where an offer for a lead magnet is presented in exchange for contact information.

For example, let's say we want to offer a free report "Top 3 Exercises for Low Back Pain" as our lead magnet.

Imagine somebody clicks on a link in an email or on a Facebook ad that says, "Anybody that is suffering from back pain might like this article or might like this report. These exercises can help you get pain relief from home in under 10 minutes. Click here to download the Top 3 Exercises for Low Back Pain."

So once they click that, they go to a squeeze page.

The squeeze page is made up of a headline, usually an image of what the prospect will get in exchange for their contact information, either some bullets or a video to describe the benefits the prospect will get from the lead magnet (and maybe addressing objections), and lastly a call to action with a form where the prospect can enter their contact info.

Then, when the person enters their email, they are taken to the content, the free video in this case.

Now you have their contact information.

You may be thinking... Why not send them straight to my website? What's the difference?

Well a squeeze page does not have a menu, it does not have any other links, when you're on a squeeze page you have only 2 choices... One, enter your information for the lead magnet OR two, leave the page.

What are we competing with on the internet?

Attention, distraction, lots of options. A squeeze page takes those options away and focuses your prospect on one thing only. Your call to action.

This makes a squeeze page have a much higher conversion rate than the homepage of your website.

The pages we've built for clients generally convert from between 25% to 75% of people who land on the page. The average for a homepage is not even close to that.

So once you have their contact information, what can and MUST we do?

Follow up!

It's a very common mistake that owners make to assume once someone is interested, they're pretty much going to become a patient. Huge mistake.

People are generally programmed to say NO initially. They have their guard up, especially with cold traffic, and need to get to know, like, and trust you first. Also, they need to believe you can take them from where they are today (with back pain, neck pain, etc.) to where they want to be.

So from here you MUST follow up.

How?

There are some simple ways I'm sure you know (but believe it or not, most people don't even bother to do them).

1 - Call them
2 - Message them (text, email, etc.)

Most owners know how to do this manually. In the next section I'll tell you about something much more powerful. You can automatically follow up with customers using automation.

Experience has shown in working with dozens of our high end clients that automation can easily 10X your results. You are going to love this.

SECTION 7 – ADVANCED AUTOMATED PATIENT CONVERSION SYSTEMS

With what I'm about to show you, I've built an automatic patient conversion system that has attracted an average of 50 prospective patients and converted 20 patients (full POC) automatically. Here's what it looks like:

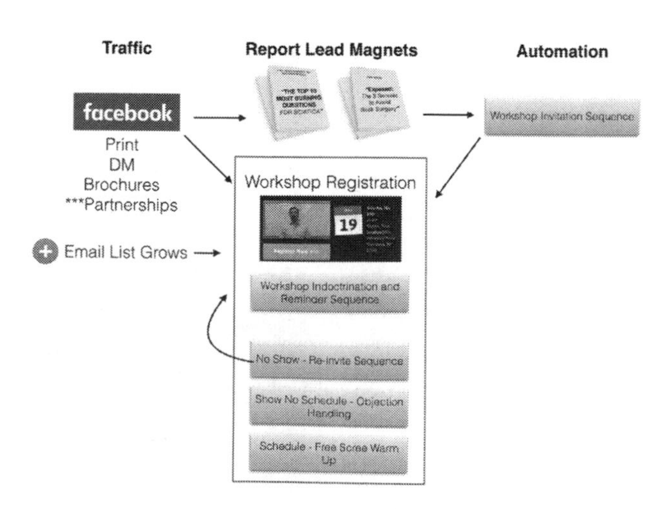

How does this work... And what does it mean...

So far you understand steps 1, 2, and 4 above... Send highly qualified traffic to lead magnets, follow-up and convert on a tripwire (through a workshop) then into a screen and a full plan of care.

But as we learned in the last chapter, what about the people who say NO to your initial offer (usually about 80%).

You can call them manually, but that would take a TON of man power. Instead, we'll use automation to both get our prospective patients to know like and true us, and to show them we can help them get from where they are today (with their pain) to where they want to be.

Let me explain in an example I've built out for Madden PT.

A prospective patient (let's call her Mary) signs up for a lead magnet which is a free report called "The Top Burning Questions For Sciatica Sufferers".

After Mary signs up, we have her phone number and email address.

Someone at Madden PT is notified, and they call Mary, but are not able to get through.

This is where the magic happens.

Since Mary signed up for a report on sciatica, we can assume she is suffering from some sort of lower back pain.

Using automation software, we can automatically send emails to Mary with useful information about lower back pain, what could be causing her issues, and how she can get better without her objections. The content we provide will show her we understand what she's going through, help her understand how she can get from where she is today, to where she wants to be, and build a ton of goodwill in the process.

So what we'll do with Mary after we deliver the report is send a series of content (we like to use video for added know, like, trust)... Everyone building good will and delivering value, and every one making a useful offer.

Here's an example in a timeline:

Day 1: Mary signs up and gets sciatica report.

Day 2: We automatically send Mary an email with a link to a video about the most common causes of back pain with an offer to come to our next Lower Back Pain and Sciatica Workshop at the end. Mary watches the video, but does not take us up on the offer yet.

Day 3: We automatically send Mary another email, this time with a link to a video showing her some exercises she can do for some relief. This time Mary watches the video and sees our offer at the end to come to the workshop. She registers because one of the exercises helped her.

Day 4: Through the workshop date: We send Mary a series of what we call Indoctrination emails that both teach her more stuff, get more goodwill, and remind her of the workshop at the same time.

Day of the Workshop: Mary shows up excited to see the person who's been teaching her all this useful stuff in the videos, and signs up for a free screen. Attends a few days later, and then a full plan of care.

Notice what happened here... We had 3 opportunities to convert Mary and she didn't convert until the 3rd one. In reality, most people still won't convert at this point. Which is why we extend this type of email series and goodwill series indefinitely (but not always emails everyday).

Once we did get Mary to sign up for our workshop, we did not stop there.

She was still not converted into a full plan of care. So we send even more goodwill for the purpose of helping Mary and getting her to show up to the workshop.

All this happened automatically.

And it doesn't stop there... We can setup automated email sequences to convert patients who suffer from any type of pain... The same thing can happen for neck, shoulder, knee, etc...

Any place where people have an opportunity to drop off, we can (and do) support with automation. Warming people up for free screens, during their plan of care (increase show up, compliance, and deliver better care), and afterwards to get them to refer friends (return path).

All of this requires a ton of work, so how do we build this all out?

You've got 2 choices:

1. If you're super tech savvy and love to geek out on stuff like this, you can study it. I'm putting together a free web class on the basics and showing resources to learn more. You can register for free at **KillerMarketingSecretsBook.com/Resources**

2. If you want to save the time and get a shortcut, we put together a very exclusive product that does all of this for you. Chad and I spent lots of time and over $2 million in advertising and training to learn what works. We've built it and tested it in over 30 practices (as of March 2016). You can get all of it in about 2 weeks if you are a fit for the program. I'm going to be upfront about this, this is NOT for you if you're looking for a cheap solution. This is only for practice owners super serious who want to dominate their market. If you think that might be you, go to **KillerMarketingSecretsBook.com/Resources** to submit an application.

ACTION GUIDE

To conclude this, I want to talk about something more advanced and bring it all together.

Here's a quick action guide:

1. Remember the fundamentals. Pay attention to your market, message, media, match (especially the media in this case) and ALWAYs lead with value and make useful offers that have value built into them.
2. Start with some simple email marketing. Send lead magnets with soft offers to your past patient list. Go to **KillerMarketingSecretsBook.com/Resources** for a list of email tools.
3. Put up Facebook posts that are valuable to the hot and warm audiences I recommend, and always include a call to action at the end.
4. If you loved this chapter and want to explode your new patient flow, go to **KillerMarketingSecretsBook.com/Resources** to register for a free course to learn more OR apply for our exclusive automatic patient automation product at **KillerMarketingSecretsBook.com/Resources.**

Special Invitation for Private Practice PT Owners ONLY

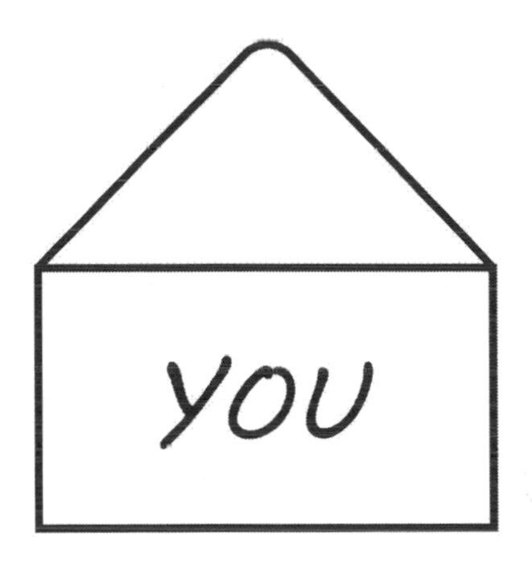

Fed up with POPTS competition? Hospital Systems buying your referral sources? National corporate PT companies moving in on your home turf?

Whether you're a small solo practice who's just starting out...or you're an established All-star or Hall of Fame practice owner who wants to stay ahead of the healthcare changes and take your practice to the next level...

Join over 275 other Private Practice Owners in the US, Canada, Australia and Malaysia who've completed the Killer Marketing Training...and are in the BPTM Secret Community...

In the Killer Marketing Training, you'll learn:

- **How to "Fix Your Funnel"...and the 4 Key Systems to Fix BEFORE You Invest in Marketing Your Private Practice...**
- **How to Efficiently and Effectively Build a System to Communicate With Your Past Patients So You Increase Your Marketing ROI by Attracting More Past Patients AND More Word of Mouth...**
- **How to Market to 383 Local Referral Sources in Less Than 60 Minutes Each Month...**
- **How to Host Killer Workshops That Attract Patients You Want to Treat Without Relying on Physician Referrals...**

The Killer Marketing Training is Now Bigger and Better...

When I first started hosting the Killer Marketing Training, it was simply me sharing what's working here at Madden PT...

That has now evolved into a network of successful private practice owners supporting each other in building, implementing and testing these systems...

Resulting in HUGE Wins Private Practice Owners...

Our Mission

At BPTM, our team, is committed to helping and guiding 100 Private Practice Owners to DOUBLE their practice...

What's That Mean?

If you're seeing 1,000 visits/month now...that would be helping you to get to 2,000 visits/month.

If you have a $1,000,000/year Income Practice...that would be helping you get to $2,000,000/year.

Isn't That a Bit of a Stretch?

Yes. It is...

But I've seen and helped other practice owners do this first hand...and you have now too...with the right scientific systems in place...and our team here at BPTM working with private practice Owners who are hard-working and committed enough to take their practice to the next level...

Great things are happening...